I love that these men have not only created a clear and concise theology for every believer, but also that they are disciple makers who seek to live out what they teach. This book will help church leaders as well as the everyday disciple maker in your church or ministry.

— **Jim Putman**, author of *Real-Life Discipleship*

A short, compelling read that invites followers of Jesus into the life-changing call to embrace Jesus' commitment to disciple making. Harrington and Sager illuminate not only the genius of Jesus' words, but just as significantly, the genius of his world-changing ways.

— **Dave Clayton**, Lead Minister of Ethos Church and Leader of Awaken Nashville

Anytime you see the name Bobby Harrington on a book, you know it will be about advancing the kingdom of God through making disciples. *Disciple Making* is another brick in the disciple making movement's wall. This work is solid, short, and foundational. This practical tool can help church leaders get on the same page. Two of our enemies are confusion and ambiguity. This work provides clarity and specificity.

— **Bill Hull**, author and founder of the Bonhoeffer Project

This thoughtful and urgent invitation will challenge the status quo, enlighten beginners, and inspire those already on the journey to becoming disciple making churches. Harrington and Sager help us develop the Spirit-driven conviction and razor-sharp biblical clarity that are essential for disciple making to move from trendy lingo to widespread reality.

— **Drew Moore**, Lead Minister, Canyon Ridge
Christian Church

All of us pastors and church leaders are having to reevaluate the way we do everything today. This book has served our church as a fantastic guide to clarify, recapture, and align ourselves to the life-giving but often missed mission of Jesus.

— **Nate Ross**, Lead Pastor, Northside
Christian Church

Every organization faces mission drift—even churches! We see all around us the results of this drift: lukewarm Christians, dying churches, and fruitless believers. Bobby Harrington and Scott Sager have written a valuable tool to reorient us to be mission-true churches. *Disciple Making* is theologically sound, concisely written, and immensely practical. When read, believed, and applied, it will play a key role in stopping the drift!

— **Buddy Bell**, Lead Minister, Landmark
Church of Christ

In a time when many churches seem to be searching for a mission, this book by Bobby and Scott on disciple making makes it clear that we don't have to write a mission for the church. Jesus already has. Making disciple making the main thing will focus the church, declutter the church, energize the church, and fill the church with the power of the Spirit. This book will help you and your church find the unique mission that Jesus gave you.

— **David Youn**g, author of *A Grand Illusion*
and *King Jesus and the Beauty of Obedience-Based
Discipleship*

Emerging from the experience of COVID, church leaders have seen the church exposed by the pandemic in stark and convicting ways. *Disciple Making* provides clear, succinct, passionate, and scriptural re-visioning of the non-negotiable purpose of every church—namely, to make multiplying disciples, period. By addressing the *why* as well as the *what* and *how*, Harrington and Sager provide perfect motivational fuel for the disciple making engine of and the change-agents in your church.

— **John Wasem**, Advancement Director, Stadia Church Planting

Bobby Harrington and Scott Sager have provided an encouraging and motivating source. This practical and studious approach has further encouraged me in the work of leading the church's "core mission." It has fortified my motivation to continuously inspire others to be disciple makers as well.

— **Robert Gardenhire**, Senior Minister, Schrader Lane Church of Christ

I have been convinced for quite some time that today's church desperately needs to focus on the basics of the faith. Too often the church gets caught up in multiple activities and ministries and forgets their primary purpose. What could be more important than recovering the essential focus of the church—making disciples? This book is a needed and helpful tool for church leaders and members to recommit to this primary calling of the church.

— **Earl Lavender**, Director of Missional Studies, Hazelip School of Theology, Lipscomb University

BOBBY HARRINGTON
& W. SCOTT SAGER

THE REAL LIFE THEOLOGY SERIES

DISCIPLE MAKING

THE CORE MISSION
OF THE CHURCH

8

RENƎW.org

Disciple Making: The Core Mission of the Church
Copyright © 2021 by Bobby Harrington & W. Scott Sager

Requests for information should be sent via e-mail to Renew. Visit Renew.org for contact information.

All Scripture quotations, unless otherwise indicated, are taken from the Holy Bible, New International Version®, NIV®. Copyright © 1973, 1978, 1984, 2011 by Biblica, Inc.® Used by permission of Zondervan. All rights reserved worldwide. www.zondervan. com. The "NIV" and "New International Version" are trademarks registered in the United States Patent and Trademark Office by Biblica, Inc.®

Scripture quotations marked ESV are from the ESV® Bible (The Holy Bible, English Standard Version®). Copyright © 2001 by Crossway, a publishing ministry of Good News Publishers. Used by permission. All rights reserved.

Italics have been added to Scripture quotations by the author.

Any Internet addresses (websites, blogs, etc.) in this book are offered as a resource. They are not intended in any way to be or imply an endorsement by Renew.org, nor does Renew.org vouch for the content of these sites and contact numbers for the life of this book.

All rights reserved. No part of this book, including icons and images, may be reproduced in any manner without prior written permission from the copyright holder, except where noted in the text and in the case of brief quotations embodied in critical articles and reviews.

ISBN (paperback) 978-1-949921-75-5
ISBN (Mobi) 978-1-949921-76-2
ISBN (ePub) 978-1-949921-77-9

Cover and interior design by Harrington Interactive Media (harringtoninteractive.com)

Printed in the United States of America

CONTENTS

GENERAL
EDITOR'S NOTE

God desires disciple making to be a key focus for the local church because he wants more than just "Christians": he wants disciples of Jesus. At the Renew.org Network, we like to say God wants disciples who make disciples and who plant disciple making churches. This fulfills the vision of heaven in Revelation 7:9:

> I looked, and there before me was a great multitude
> that no one could count, from every nation, tribe,
> people and language, standing before the throne
> and before the Lamb.

The purpose of this short book is to make the scriptural case that disciple making is the core mission of the local church.

Bobby Harrington and Scott Sager both currently serve as lead ministers/pastors of local churches. They are engaged daily in the practical implications and nuts-and-bolts reality to which they point in this book.

Bobby is the founding and lead pastor of Harpeth Christian Church (Franklin, Tennessee). He is the CEO of both Renew.org and Discipleship.org, national disciple making networks. He has degrees from Harding University and a Doctor of Ministry from The Southern Baptist Theological Seminary. He is the author or co-author of more than a dozen books on disciple making.

Scott is the lead minister at The Green Hills Church in Nashville, Tennessee, and a vice president of Lipscomb University, teaching for its College of Bible and Ministry. Scott recently published *Jesus in Isolation: Lazarus, Viruses, and Us*. He founded Christ's Family Ministries and serves with several charities. He earned degrees from Abilene Christian University and a Doctor of Ministry from Southern Methodist University.

This book expounds on the section from the Renew.org Leaders' Faith Statement called "Disciple Making":

> We believe the core mission of the local church is making disciples of Jesus Christ—it is God's plan "A" to redeem the world and manifest the reign of

his kingdom. We want to be disciples who make disciples because of our love for God and others. We personally seek to become more and more like Jesus through his Spirit so that Jesus would live through us. To help us focus on Jesus, his sacrifice on the cross, our unity in him, and his coming return, we typically share communion in our weekly gatherings. We desire the fruits of biblical disciple making, which are disciples who live and love like Jesus and "go" into every corner of society and to the ends of the earth. Disciple making is the engine that drives our missional service to those outside the church. We seek to be known where we live for the good that we do in our communities. We love and serve all people, as Jesus did, no strings attached. At the same time, as we do good for others, we also seek to form relational bridges that we prayerfully hope will open doors for teaching people the gospel of the kingdom and the way of salvation.

*See the full Network Faith Statements at the end of this book.

Support Scriptures: Matthew 28:19–20; Galatians 4:19; Acts 2:41; Philippians 1:20–21; Colossians 1:27–29; 2 Corinthians 3:3;

1 Thessalonians 2:19–20; John 13:34–35;
1 John 3:16; 1 Corinthians 13:1–13;
Luke 22:14–23; 1 Corinthians 11:17–24; Acts 20:7.

The following tips might help you use this book more effectively (and the other books in the *Real Life Theology* series):

1. *Five questions, answers, and Scriptures.* We framed this book around five key questions with five short answers and five notable Scriptures. This format provides clarity, making it easier to commit crucial information to memory. This format also enables the books in the *Real Life Theology* series to support our catechism. Our catechism is a series of fixed questions and answers for instruction in church or home. In all, the series has fifty-two questions, answers, and key Scriptures. This particular book focuses on the five that are most pertinent to disciple making.
2. *Personal reflection.* At the end of each chapter are six reflection questions. Each chapter is short and intended for everyday people to read and then process. The questions help you to engage the specific teachings and, if you prefer, to journal your practical reflections.

3. *Discussion questions.* The reflection questions double as discussion-group questions. Even if you do not write down the answers, the questions can be used to stimulate group conversation.

4. *Summary videos.* You can find three to seven-minute video teachings that summarize the book, as well as each chapter, at Renew.org. These short videos can function as standalone teachings. But for groups or group leaders using the book, they can also be used to launch discussion of the reading.

May God use this book to fuel faithful and effective disciple making in your life and church.

For King Jesus,

Daniel McCoy

Co-General Editor, *Real Life Theology* series

INTRODUCTION

> The Church exists for nothing else but to draw men
> into Christ, to make them little Christs. If they are
> not doing that, all the cathedrals, clergy, missions,
> sermons, even the Bible itself, are simply a waste
> of time. God became Man for no other purpose.
> — C. S. Lewis

In this book, we teach you the basics of disciple making and encourage you to make it a core focus of your life. We believe disciple making is the core mission of the church and that C. S. Lewis got it right when he said, "The Church exists for nothing else but to draw men into Christ, to make them little Christs."[1] Making "little Christs" is another way of saying "disciple making."

Being clear with definitions is important, so let's begin with our definition of disciple making:

> *Disciple making is entering into relationships to intentionally help people follow Jesus, be changed by Jesus, and join the mission of Jesus.*[2]

Although Jesus officially comes onto the scene in the New Testament, disciple making is a common theme throughout the whole Bible. Disciple making was God's preferred method long before it became the church's core mission. Let's start with an important Old Testament passage, where God taught disciple making to parents when he formed the nation of Israel.

THE MASTER PLAN FOR DISCIPLE MAKING IN THE OLD TESTAMENT

WHILE THE OLD TESTAMENT contains many examples of disciple making, one key section in Deuteronomy captures it best. We must not overlook this passage because it is the central passage of Judaism even to this day. When God (through Moses and his disciple, Joshua) led the people of Israel out of Egypt and into the Promised Land, he established a core method for disciple making for families. By this method, the Israelites would learn to love God, know his ways through Scripture, and obey him.

The key verses are from Deuteronomy 6:4–9, and the Israelites deemed them so important that they incorporated the verses into a prayer called the *Shema*,[3] which they later required to be recited *daily* and in the synagogue as formative to living a life that both pursues and pleases God. You can think of this passage as the Great Commission *before* the Great Commission of Jesus in Matthew 28:18–20 (a passage we will explain in greater detail in Chapter 1). This earlier Great Commission offers the core method by which the Old Testament people of Israel made disciples and also offered the relational framework of disciple making that Jesus himself would utilize centuries later when he chose his first disciples. This method is intentional, relational transformation (more on this description below). Notice how the *Shema* begins:

> Hear, O Israel: The LORD our God, the LORD is one. Love the LORD your God with all your heart and with all your soul and with all your strength. (Deuteronomy 6:4–5)

Moses first announced God as the unifying force behind all of creation and all of human existence—he is *one*. Allegiance to this one God requires all a person has to offer: we are to love him with our heart, soul, and strength. It is a full-bodied and relentless pursuit to know and love God. It is the core mission of God's people, Israel, so much so that the nation of Israel derives its name "Israel" from being the people "who strive and wrestle with God" (see Genesis 32:28). God wanted to create for himself a people who would struggle mightily to love him, and through loving him they would disciple their children to know and love him as well.

Passing on the faith to the next generation was so critical to Israel's budding future that Moses called parents to intentionally and sacrificially spend time relationally discipling and helping their children to know, love, and follow God. Moses then gave specific instructions to parents as the disciple makers of their children:

> These commandments that I give you today are to be on your hearts. Impress them on your children. Talk about them when you sit at home and when you walk along the road, when you lie down and when you get up. Tie them as symbols on your hands and bind them on your foreheads. Write them on the doorframes of your houses and on your gates. (Deuteronomy 6:6–9)

As we see, the one passing on faith must have a relentless and transformative pursuit of God (what we call a "God-life") as the focus of their living. That person is then to "impress" the God-life upon their children through purposively living out the faith and faith-filled instruction. These instructions show us the pursuit of

God was to be *the* topic of conversation around the house for God's people as they sat together and along the road as they traveled together. Devotion to God was to be the last thing inputted into a child's "hard drive" at night and the first thing coming out of their parent's mouth when the family rebooted again the next morning. A pursuit of God was to be evident at the entrance to the home, through the home's decor, as well as how they adorned their bodies. Parents were to be intentional, courageous, and conspicuous in their pursuit to know God.

The disciple making commission from Deuteronomy 6 begins with God first calling parents to be disciples themselves—by fully loving him with all of their heart, soul, and strength—and then it calls parents to disciple their children so they too will love God with their heart, soul, and strength.

Notice three key elements God prescribes that apply to parents both then and now:

Intentional. Parents are to be purposeful and goal-oriented. Their mission is to *impress* the teachings of God on their children so they too will love God. In God's estimation, "impressive parents" are not the ones who raise the most accomplished kids, but the ones who impress their own God-life into the moldable clay of their children's lives. It is a thorough and all-encompassing mission, from the time they "get up," until the time they "lie down" each day. This intentionality expresses itself by the use of

Scripture everywhere—on arms, foreheads, and even the doorframes of their houses. Yes, that is a lot of intentional focus! And, yes, that kind of diligence is necessary to disciple children both then and now.[4]

Relational. Parents should disciple their children in a relational way and in the normal stuff of life. The text envisions many natural conversations, for example, at home, during walks, in the mornings, and at bedtime. With their minds focused upon the discipling of children, parents constantly use the relational conversations and discussions that come up in life to integrate the teachings of God into their children's lives.

Transformation. The end goal of disciple making is to make true disciples. When children grow up with the Deuteronomy 6 disciple making model, they are very likely to grow up as those who love God with all their heart, soul, and strength. They become disciples who leave their homes to establish families of their own, where—following the example of their parents and the teaching of the *Shema*—they too are equipped to disciple their children, repeating the model generation after generation.

A careful examination of Jesus' life shows how Jesus used this same model when he made disciples as a spiritual parent. He formed his disciples through this intentional, relational process in the normal, everyday course of Jewish life in the first century. Then he commissioned his disciples to go and repeat the process by making disciples of others, doing for others what he had done for them.

> Therefore, go and make disciples of all nations, baptizing them in the name of the Father and of the Son and of the Holy Spirit, and teaching them to obey everything I have commanded you. And surely I am with you always, to the very end of the age. (Matthew 28:19–20)

Let's now turn to the teachings and life of Jesus to understand better what he meant when he commissioned his disciples to make disciples.

1

WHY ARE THE LIFE AND TEACHINGS OF JESUS IMPORTANT FOR DISCIPLE MAKING?

Answer: Jesus shows us by his life and teachings how we should live as his disciples.

Therefore go and make disciples of all nations, baptizing them in the name of the Father and of the Son and of the Holy Spirit, and teaching them to obey everything I have commanded you. And surely I am with you always, to the very end of the age.
— Matthew 28:19–20

The Christian world emphasizes Christmas and Easter, the two most prominent holidays on the Christian calendar. These two days focus on the incarnation (how God became flesh in baby Jesus) and the death, burial, and resurrection (how God forgives our sins). Along with the emphasis on these two days, a lot of theology focuses on these two points about Jesus too. Preachers regularly emphasize how Jesus was 100 percent human and divine and that he died and rose from the dead to forgive us of our sins (and provide us with heaven). These two focal points are good and true, but isolated from the rest of the Gospels, they do not provide enough emphasis on what happened between Jesus' birth and resurrection.

To follow the Bible truly, we must also focus on the teachings and life of Jesus.

If we exclude this middle focus, we can inadvertently create a *transactional gospel*, in which the call is simply to place our faith in Jesus' identity and cross (the human part of "the deal"), and then God will forgive our sins (God's part of the deal). That gospel—if we are not careful—simply becomes a transaction. By excluding what it means to follow Jesus' teachings and imitate his life, we share a gospel not taught in the Word of God.

God calls us to more than a transaction.

God calls us to become disciples of Jesus.

This is why we need to know Jesus and his teachings. This focus was made clear at the end of Jesus' **GOD CALLS US TO BECOME DISCIPLES OF JESUS.** time on earth when he gave the Great Commission to his disciples.

> All authority in heaven and on earth has been given to me. Therefore go and make disciples of all nations, baptizing them in the name of the Father and of the Son and of the Holy Spirit, and teaching them to obey everything I have commanded you. And surely I am with you always, to the very end of the age. (Matthew 28:18b–20)

These are Jesus' final words—and that fact alone makes them important. But they are more than just final words: they are Jesus' final mission to his disciples and the expression of God's heart for everyone on earth.

Jesus wants disciples.

And Jesus wants his disciples to make more disciples.

Many people mistakenly think that the Great Commission is about conversions. But that is not what the text says. It is about conversation and living as disciples. The text says that disciple making includes baptizing people and teaching them to obey all Jesus' teachings and trust his presence until the end. Jesus' master plan for his disciples was to reach the whole world by making other disciples.

It is that simple.

Notice two crucial descriptions of how we are to teach as we disciple people. First, Jesus did not tell his disciples just to baptize and share information. He instructed them to teach *obedience* to his commands ("teaching them to obey"). Second, Jesus taught his disciples to teach obedience to *everything he commanded* ("to obey everything I have commanded you"). As David Young points out in his wonderful book on this topic, Jesus commanded *obedience-based disciple making*. That is the type of disciple making God wants us to uphold today.[5] We are to obey everything Jesus commanded.

This short book is a part of the *Real Life Theology* series that focuses on how we can know and obey everything that Jesus commands as disciples.[6] Our main goal is to show that disciple making—which involves helping people in every nation come to Jesus for both salvation and transformation—is the core mission of the church. Before we focus directly on how and why we make disciples, let's see why the teachings and life of Jesus form the core curriculum in disciple making.

JESUS' TEACHINGS ARE OUR CURRICULUM FOR DISCIPLE MAKING.

JESUS' TEACHINGS

Jesus claimed that following his teachings was foundational for living life as it was intended: "I am the light of the world. Whoever follows me will never walk in darkness, but will have the light of life" (John 8:12). Jesus described himself and his teachings this way:

> I have come into the world as a light, so that no one who believes in me should stay in darkness. If anyone hears my words but does not keep them, I do not judge that person. For I did not come to judge the world, but to save the world. *There is a judge for the one who rejects me and does not accept my words; the very words I have spoken will condemn them at the last day.* For I did not speak on my own, but the Father who sent me commanded me to say all that I have spoken. I know that his command leads to eternal life. So whatever I say is just what the Father has told me to say. (John 12:46–50)

Elsewhere Jesus compared his words and teachings to the foundation of a house. Merely claiming to follow him and doing great things in his name will not be enough on the day of judgment. Rather, only those who truly build their lives on his teachings will enter the kingdom of heaven.

> Not everyone who says to me, "Lord, Lord," will enter the kingdom of heaven, but only the one who does the will of my Father who is in heaven. Many will say to me on that day, "Lord, Lord, did we not prophesy in your name and in your name drive out demons and in your name perform many miracles?" Then I will tell them plainly, "I never knew you. Away from me, you evildoers!" *Therefore everyone who hears these words of mine and puts them into practice is like a wise man who built his house on the rock.* (Matthew 7:21–24)

Jesus makes it clear: our adherence to his teachings will be the basis by which God will evaluate our lives.

Just before his ascension back to heaven, Jesus committed his words and teachings to his apostles (Matthew 28:18–20). Jesus also promised that God would guide the apostles, ensuring they accurately recalled everything through the Holy Spirit. Notice the following promise.

> These words you hear are not my own; they belong to the Father who sent me. All this I have spoken while still with you. *But the Advocate, the Holy Spirit, whom the Father will send in my name, will teach you all things and will remind you of everything I have said to you.* (John 14:24b–26)

According to Jesus, the Holy Spirit would ensure that the disciples be properly taught and remember everything he had told them. God did not just rely on the impressive memory practices of the ancient people. He guided them and protected the accuracy of Jesus' teachings by his Holy Spirit.

This is why the first Christians devoted themselves to the apostles' teachings: these teachings were not just inspirational thoughts but the inspired teachings of Jesus himself!

> They devoted themselves to the apostles' teaching and to fellowship, to the breaking of bread and to prayer. (Acts 2:42)

Jesus Christ's words were God's *final* message for the human race.

> In the past God spoke to our ancestors through the prophets at many times and in various ways, but in these last days he has spoken to us by his Son, whom he appointed heir of all things, and through whom he made the universe. (Hebrews 1:1–2)

As mentioned earlier, at a basic level, a disciple is a student, apprentice, learner. So, yes, at a basic level we look to Jesus as a teacher. Yet Jesus calls us to a much higher level of devotion than we typically give the teachings we study. He calls us to *live out* the teachings of his kingdom. These teachings are our curriculum for disciple making. Thankfully, however, Jesus gives us more than just teachings and an expectation to live according to them. He also gives us *himself* as the model to follow.

JESUS' LIFE

THE GOSPEL OF MARK describes how Jesus began his ministry by calling people into God's kingdom reign (Mark 1:14–18). A prominent focus of Jesus' teachings was describing what this kingdom was like. Take, for example, Jesus' kingdom parables in Matthew 13. Jesus also spent much of his time describing how to live life as citizens of God's kingdom. For example, the countercultural ethics of the Sermon on the Mount confront every reader with the radical righteousness that characterizes kingdom life.

Yet as the Gospel of Mark describes, Jesus did more than just invite people to follow his teachings about the kingdom. His invitation into the kingdom involved following *him*. He used words that described a total lifestyle renovation, such as "repent" (turning from evil and turning back to God) and "believe" (from the Greek word *pistis,* which entails more than mental assent to an idea; in royal contexts, it often denotes allegiance to a king).[7]

> Jesus went into Galilee, proclaiming the good news of God. "The time has come," he said. "The *kingdom of God* has come near. *Repent* and *believe* the good news!" As Jesus walked beside the Sea of Galilee, he saw Simon and his brother Andrew casting a net into the lake, for they were fishermen. "Come, *follow me*," Jesus said, "and I will send you out to fish for people." At once they left their nets and followed him. (Mark 1:14–18)

Notice how the explicit invitation came to two brothers, Peter and Andrew, casting their nets on the Sea of Galilee, "for they were fishermen" (Mark 1:16). Jesus offered them a front row seat to his life and teachings if they would follow him. These two career fishermen made their livelihoods from the sea. But now Jesus was asking them to drop their nets and set off with him into his kingdom waters to cast spiritual nets that would capture the hearts of men and women everywhere.

This invitation to leave a familiar source of income was a lot for Jesus to ask. But we learn an important focus: don't focus on what you are walking away from, but on whom you are walking toward. The text tells us "at once" they dropped their nets and entered into the greatest adventure anyone has ever known (Mark 1:18). They had found more than a body of information worth learning; they had discovered a life worth following.

Jesus gave us a life to imitate. Whether we are male or female, Jew or Greek, rich or poor—the more we look like Jesus, the more we become our truest self, the self for which God created us. Jesus is the model for what it looks like to live as God intends. Because of this, we are to follow after Jesus by walking in his steps. John described it poignantly: "Whoever claims to live in him must live as Jesus did" (1 John 2:6).

This is why the expression "Follow me" was one of Jesus' favorite invitations (Matthew 4:19; 8:22; 9:9; 10:38; 16:24; 19:21). He explained to his disciples, "The student is not above the teacher, but everyone who is fully trained will be like their teacher" (Luke 6:40). For example, notice how Jesus pointed to his own example when teaching about love.

> A new command I give you: Love one another. As I have loved you, so you must love one another. By this everyone will know that you are my disciples, if you love one another. (John 13:34–35)

Jesus demonstrated what it meant to love sacrificially, and then held up his example to define love in his teaching.

Jesus' life is our example, model, and the one we imitate. For example, suffering is a common challenge that we face when we are disciples. How do we handle something like that? Peter explains our need to have Jesus as our model in suffering in 1 Peter 2:21–23.

> To this you were called, because Christ suffered for you, leaving you an example, that you should follow in his steps. "He committed no sin, and no deceit was found in his mouth." When they hurled their insults at him, he did not retaliate; when he suffered, he made no threats. Instead, he entrusted himself to him who judges justly.

There are so many situations in life and God wants us to respond to each of them as disciples of Jesus. Yet the Word of God does not tell—nor could it tell us—how to handle each situation. Instead, Scripture focuses on the underlying principles. As God inspires Paul, he urges Christians to *imitate the mindset of Jesus.*

> Have the same mindset as Christ Jesus: Who, being in very nature God, did not consider equality with God something to be used to his own advantage; rather, he made himself nothing by taking the very nature of a servant, being made in human likeness. (Philippians 2:5–7)

TEACHINGS AND MODEL

Between the incarnation of Jesus and his death and resurrection, we find crucial curriculum for disciple making. For in Jesus' teachings and life we learn how to live as disciples of Jesus. As pivotal as the cross and resurrection are to our salvation, we must not skip over the bulk of the Gospels and the teachings of the apostles in defining what it means to be a disciple of Jesus. His disciples hold up his teachings and life as central to their calling as Christians.

Yet the point can be stated even more strongly. Jesus' teachings and life provide us with more than just important content in our disciple making curriculum. They also demonstrate the best way to *communicate* that content. Put another way, Jesus gives us both our teaching *and model* for disciple making. For when we study how Jesus taught and lived, we see a life-on-life method for making disciples far more transformational than mere instruction in a classroom.[8]

Just as the Israelites discipled their children to grow up and disciple their children in turn, so Jesus discipled a group of twelve men who matured and then went out to repeat the process. Jesus' intentional, relational transformation is a disciple making process, and it is the ideal plan by which people from every nation, language, and tribe will come to be disciples (Revelation 7:9) and fulfill the Great Commission. Our next step is to focus on Jesus' teachings more precisely with the aim to define what exactly it means to be a disciple of Jesus.

REFLECTION & DISCUSSION QUESTIONS

1. How would you explain to someone that it is a weakness if we emphasize only the birth, death, burial, and resurrection of Jesus?

_____

_____

_____

_____

2. Read Matthew 7:21–24. Why is it important both to understand Jesus' teachings and put them into practice?

_____

_____

_____

_____

_____

3. What kind of life change was involved when Peter and Andrew responded to the invitation of Jesus to repent, believe, and follow him (Mark 1:14–18)? Why is that invitation still fundamentally important today?

_____

_____

_____

_____

_____

4. When we describe the kingdom of God as the realm in which Jesus reigns or rules, what comes to mind? How can we invite Jesus' kingdom reign and rule more fully into our lives?

_____

_____

_____

_____

_____

5. What does it mean to develop the same mindset as Jesus Christ (Philippians 2:5–7)? What is the best way to develop that mindset?

6. How has Jesus transformed your life?

2

WHAT IS A DISCIPLE OF JESUS?

Answer: A disciple of Jesus is someone who is following Jesus, being changed by Jesus, and is committed to the mission of Jesus.

And Jesus said to them, "Follow me, and I will make you become fishers of men."
— Mark 1:17, ESV

(Bobby) became friends with Larry as we watched our sons play hockey together. Larry happily accepted my invitation to join a Bible discussion group. Through this discussion group, it became clear Larry knew nothing about the Bible. Growing up in a rough New York community, he had experienced trauma at the early age of twelve, when he saw a member of the mafia kill his father. It so traumatized him that he spent the next thirty-plus years of his life keeping himself far from conversations about death—and ultimately about God. Yet because of this new friendship, he was getting into the Bible—and learning a lot too.

One day, Larry described to a co-worker what he was learning about the Bible. In response, the man questioned and challenged Larry's new realizations about God, Jesus, and the Bible. Returning to our Bible study confused and seeking clarity, Larry wanted to be sure this new path would be worth it.

"Bottom line," he asked me, "what is it all about?" He wanted to know the point of life and how Jesus fit in. People have always asked questions like this in various ways: *Why am I here? What is God's purpose for my life? Where is my life going? How does it all end?* These were probably the same questions Adam and Eve had asked God during their daily visits in the Garden of Eden, and people are still seeking answers to them in our day.

I gave Larry a quick answer: "God wants a relationship with you, in which you become a disciple of Jesus." This bottom-line, one-sentence response didn't include a warning about hell (although I was concerned about that for him), or the reality of life after death in general (even though that is important), or that he would need to follow the teachings of the Bible (which developing a relationship with God requires). There was time for those things. He needed to know, bottom line, what it was all about, and I told him it's all about *being a disciple of Jesus.* It included receiving both salvation in Jesus and transformation into the image of Jesus. That is what God wants for all of us. He wants everyone in the world—of "every nation, tribe, people and language" (Revelation 7:9)—to become a disciple of Jesus Christ.

So what exactly *is* a disciple?

A BIBLICAL DEFINITION OF A DISCIPLE

LINGUISTICALLY, THE WORD FOR "disciple" in the Greek is *mathētēs*, and, although we translate it "disciple," it also means learner, student, or follower. This word is most akin to the environment of an internship where an expert apprentices a student toward competency in a trade or skill. This relationship involves knowledge but focuses upon applying that knowledge to everyday situations of life to equip the learner with wisdom. The hope is that the apprentice in a trade will be the master-teacher of others in the years to come.

In addition to the linguistic route, we could also answer the question, "What is a disciple?" by looking at the descriptions of disciples of Jesus found in the New Testament. Taking our cue from various Bible passages (e.g., John 13:13; Galatians 4:19; 1 John 2:6), we discover a disciple is someone who:

- Trusts Jesus so much they pledge their full allegiance (called "faith") in him,
- Imitates Jesus' life completely as both their teacher and Lord,
- Looks to Jesus' teachings as the basis of moral decision-making,
- Loves Jesus so much that love spills over into every other relationship as well, and
- Forms their life around Jesus Christ.

Does that feel overwhelming? Don't lose heart. Instead, slow down and return to the simple-yet-radical call of Jesus to follow him. Those of us who regularly help churches learn to focus on disciple making have learned that people need a practical, specific, and memorable definition of a disciple.

We offer here a definition of a disciple that makes sense of (and room for) all the important descriptions of kingdom living we just listed. It's based on Jesus' invitation to Peter and Andrew that we discussed in the last chapter.

> And Jesus said to them, "Follow me, and
> I will make you become fishers of men."
> (Mark 1:17, ESV)

In this single verse, we find three elements of what it means to be a disciple.

- Following Jesus ("Follow me"),
- Being changed by Jesus ("and I will make you become"), and
- Joining Jesus' mission ("fishers of men").

This framework is the basis by which thousands of church leaders working with the Renew.org Network have adopted the following definition of a disciple.

> A disciple is someone who is following Jesus, being changed by Jesus, and is committed to the mission of Jesus.[9]

Mark did not include Mark 1:17 for the purpose of defining a disciple, but it serves as a helpful framework for understanding what it means to be a disciple. Everything the New Testament teaches about being a disciple can be categorized under these three elements.[10] Let's look at the three parts.

Following Jesus. Read through the New Testament and you will find the word "Christian" used only 3 times. Look for the word "disciple," though, and it shows up 296 times in the NIV. This means the English word "disciple" shows up 99 times more often than the word "Christian." While some people today might read Jesus' command to follow him in Mark 1:17 and Matthew 28:18–20 and assume it to be only for the Twelve and not for modern-day believers, that is simply a false narrative. Jesus calls us to salvation with a desire to "obey everything" Jesus commanded.

That obedience, by the way, includes the command to make disciples (Matthew 28:19–20). In this way, Jesus' original call extends to everyone to follow Jesus as a lifelong learner—to the very end of the age—and also to help make disciples and become disciple makers.

Being Changed by Jesus. Second, as we follow Jesus, we change. The New Testament promises that, as we pursue God's glory, the Holy Spirit transforms us into his image (2 Corinthians 3:18). When Jesus told Peter and Andrew, "I will make you become" (Mark 1:17, ESV), he was promising core

AS WE FOLLOW JESUS, WE CHANGE.

transformation. And as we read the disciples' stories, that's precisely what we see.

For example, take James and John who left their father, the nets, and the hired hands to follow Jesus. What kind of character did these men have when Jesus called them? Mark's Gospel tells us Jesus gave them a nickname "Sons of Thunder" (Mark 3:17). This means that their father, Zebedee, was a hothead or that they were hotheads, or both. We discover that James and John had a dark streak inside them that wanted to destroy their enemies.

Their anger and rage boiled to the surface one day in a region called Samaria, a region of half-Jews who hated the Jews as much as the Jews hated them. When the Samaritans snubbed Jesus and his band of apostles, James and John's anger boiled over, and they asked Jesus, "Do you want us to call fire down from heaven to destroy them?" (Luke 9:54). Jesus rebuked them for their suggestion, but did not exclude them from the group. In today's "cancel culture," James and John would have been shamed, shunned, and shuttled out the door for their inbuilt dislike of Samaritans. But instead of canceling them, Jesus saw that the two brothers needed more training from him and pulled them closer and strove even more to impress on them his God-life. Amazingly, by the end of his life, the elderly John was known not as a "Son of Thunder," but as the Apostle of

Love, having referenced love in his Gospel and first letter (1 John) more than any other New Testament writer.

WHEN PEOPLE FOLLOW JESUS, *JESUS* CHANGES THEM.

Our world tells us, "People don't change," and although that may be true, when people follow Jesus, *Jesus* changes them.

Joining Jesus' Mission. Third, the change Jesus works into our lives leads us to model our entire lives after Jesus, which includes our commitment to join him and "fish for people." In this, we learn to make disciples as Jesus made disciples. After all, if we obey everything Jesus commanded, that means we too will learn to replicate the process by which we became his disciples. To be a mature disciple of Jesus is to become a disciple maker like Jesus as well. It is a natural process: we follow Jesus, we are changed by Jesus, and—as we follow the one who spent 65–90 percent of his time making disciples—we too commit to make disciples as he did.[11] Loving people as Jesus loved people through service means that we want to see people come to faith in Jesus and embrace God's kingdom rule in their lives (John 13:34). Because we love people and want God's best for them, we want to help them become disciples and grow as disciples.

With our definition of a disciple in mind, with its three elements, a follow-up question is in order. Every one of us should ponder the question, *Am I a disciple of*

Jesus? Answering this question calls for more deliberation than, *Where do I go to church?* Or, *When did I get saved?* Whether or not you are a disciple of Jesus has strong implications for how you live *today*, not just for a decision made years ago.

IS BEING A DISCIPLE OPTIONAL?

In Scripture, the concept of being a disciple is not an add-on to conversion; it is part of conversion. An adage says, "What you win them with is what you win them to," and if people are won over only to the obvious benefits of salvation—say, forgiveness of sins and an eternity in heaven—then we cannot expect them to become the kind of disciples who "deny themselves and take up their cross daily and follow [Jesus]" (Luke 9:23). We must, therefore, be clear and upfront about the call to become a disciple: the Word of God teaches that the decision to receive Christ's salvation is also a decision to follow the path of discipleship found in the Bible.

Consider the following analogy: Whenever a newborn enters this world, immediately upon arrival, a nurse administers a simple health test called the "Apgar"—assessing the new baby's health with five basic criteria. A nurse will check the newborn's color, heart rate, reflexes, muscle tone, and respiration. They conduct this test not because a healthy birth is the end goal of every child or parent but because a healthy birth is only the beginning of their life—and they need to ensure the baby begins well. A healthy birth is the best indicator of a healthy life to follow.

A spiritual birth is the same: When a person makes the decision to embrace Jesus fully as both Savior and King, they enter into a spiritual new birth best seen as the coming together of five elements: faith, repentance, baptism, the reception of the Holy Spirit, and the forgiveness of sins. When these five elements come together into one single decision, together they become a fierce commitment to live for Jesus. Just as with the Apgar test at physical birth, having all five elements fully functioning in a new spiritual birth makes for the healthiest outcome.

The apostle Paul describes our new birth with a focus on water baptism this way:

> Or don't you know that all of us who were baptized into Christ Jesus were baptized into his death? We were therefore buried with him through baptism into death in order that, just as Christ was raised from the dead through the glory of the Father, we too may live a new life . . . . In the same way, count yourselves dead to sin but alive to God in Christ Jesus. (Romans 6:3–4, 11)

Baptism imitates the death, burial, and resurrection of Jesus: the person's old self dies and is buried, and the person rises up from the waters committed to a "new life." In that new life, they learn what it means to be dead to sin and "alive to God in Christ Jesus."

But here's our main point: baptism no more serves as the ultimate moment of the Christian life than the Apgar test serves as the ultimate moment of a person's human existence—it is only the start of a new life! A healthy spiritual birth launches the follower of Jesus fully and freely into the life of a disciple. Faith gives them wings to fly, repentance removes the hindrances of flight, baptism is the moment of leaving the nest, the Holy Spirit allows the believer to spread wings, and with the commitment to soar into the life intended for them—the rich life of a disciple of Jesus.

As each person remembers the day of their physical birth, spiritual followers also remember their baptism—but not as the day they checked a box, completed a transaction, or completed an exam. Rather, spiritual followers see baptism as the launching pad where they stepped out of the nest of this fallen world and soared into the great adventure of being a disciple, the life God created for them.

Now that we have looked at the definition of a disciple, we would like to explain why we are convinced that making disciples is the core mission of the church.

REFLECTION & DISCUSSION QUESTIONS

1. What are the advantages in having a clear definition of what it means to be a disciple? How can this help a church to be effective in making disciples?

_____

_____

_____

_____

_____

2. What are the three elements in this chapter from Mark 1:17 (or Matthew 4:19) that pertain to being a disciple?

_____

_____

_____

_____

_____

3. Based on the three elements in the previous question, are you a disciple of Jesus? Explain.

4. What is your reaction to using the expression, "I am a disciple of Jesus," as a more helpful expression than just saying, "I am a Christian"?

5. Why is the way we approach baptism, as described in this chapter, important for launching us into the life of being a disciple?

_____

_____

_____

_____

_____

_____

6. How would you help someone to understand that Jesus wants disciples, not just converts?

_____

_____

_____

_____

_____

_____

3

WHY IS DISCIPLE MAKING THE CORE MISSION OF THE CHURCH?

Answer: The church is God's plan to help everyone come to faith in Jesus and become more like Jesus to the glory of the Father in the power of the Spirit.

He is the one we proclaim, admonishing and teaching everyone with all wisdom, so that we may present everyone fully mature in Christ.
— Colossians 1:28

The Word of God nowhere states the mission of the church in a single verse that everyone easily agrees serves as a modern-day "mission statement." There are so many crucial tasks to which a local church in the New Testament is called that it can be difficult to bring it all down to one core mission. As an example, Rick Warren's *The Purpose Driven Church* proposes five ways to reach the ultimate purposes of the church—worship, fellowship, discipleship, ministry, and mission.[12] He connects these purposes to both the Great Commandment (Matthew 22:37–40) and the Great Commission (Matthew 28:19–20). Yet we are convinced that the five purposes Warren articulates are all expressions of one core mission that undergirds them all. We believe the underlying core mission of the church is disciple making.[13]

Consider an analogy from the sport of golf to bring together the core mission in light of the other purposes. The purpose in golf is to get a ball into a hole in the fewest strokes possible. That is how golfers keep score, and they use golf clubs to accomplish the goal of golf. The clubs are not the ultimate purpose of golf; they merely help golfers get the ball in the hole in as few strokes as possible. Similarly, the goal of disciple making is to help

THE GOAL OF DISCIPLE MAKING IS TO HELP DISCIPLES IMITATE JESUS.

disciples imitate Jesus: to follow Jesus, be changed by Jesus, and to live life in order to please Jesus. The activities of worship, fellowship, discipleship, ministry, and mission are the tools a disciple uses to realize the goal of becoming more like Jesus, and helping others do the same.

We explained in the previous chapter that disciple making includes bringing people to both salvation (into God's kingdom) and transformation (into the image of Jesus). Stated differently, God wants everyone on planet earth to be saved by Jesus and to become more and more like Jesus. In this way, becoming a disciple of Jesus— one who follows Jesus, is being changed by Jesus, and is committed to the mission of Jesus—is what life is all about. Once we are saved, growth into Christlikeness is the best way we as Jesus-followers should score ourselves.

For those in full-time ministry, there is an incredible joy and a rush of excitement that comes with beginning in a ministry role inside a local church. New leaders get excited about their roles and want to lead well, please God, and bless the people. Yet the problem most new ministers soon discover is this: their role is poorly defined. A church leader can be asked—and even expected—to play an impossible number of roles for people. Some members will think church leaders should focus on personally pastoring each member. Others will see the leaders' primary responsibility as making church run smoothly and attractively so that people keep coming. Still others will expect church leaders to be the prophetic mouthpiece for their own cultural pet peeves. It can be hard to define one's role clearly as a church leader.

So let's get specific: What exactly should happen in a local church? If we look to the Word of God, we will see that church leaders (and indeed the whole church) are tasked with this one core disciple making mission.

The apostle Paul clearly described it in his letter to the ancient church in Colossae. He reminded them that Christ is his message, and then he pointed to the goal of every church leader.

> Christ in you [is] the hope of glory. He is the one we proclaim, admonishing and teaching everyone with all wisdom, so that we may present everyone fully mature in Christ. To this end I strenuously contend with all the energy Christ so powerfully works in me. (Colossians 1:27b–29)

Paul's goal was not just proclaiming and teaching everyone about Christ. His goal—and he gave it every ounce of energy he had—was to present everyone in the church as fully mature in Christ. His goal was fully formed disciples.

The New Testament repeatedly teaches us that growth means to fundamentally focus on being formed into the image of Jesus. Paul described his own life with these words: "I have been crucified with Christ and I no longer live, but Christ lives in me" (Galatians 2:20).

Notice the following passages from the New Testament which flesh out the disciple making ministry of the church using the language of formation and transformation.

> You show that *you are a letter from Christ, the result of our ministry*, written not with ink but with the Spirit of the living God, not on tablets of stone but on tablets of human hearts. (2 Corinthians 3:3)
>
> And we all, who with unveiled faces contemplate the Lord's glory, are being *transformed into his image* with ever-increasing glory, which comes from the Lord, who is the Spirit. (2 Corinthians 3:18)
>
> My dear children, for whom I am again in the pains of childbirth *until Christ is formed in you,* how I wish I could be with you now and change my tone, because I am perplexed about you! (Galatians 4:19–20)
>
> Those God foreknew he also predestined *to be conformed to the likeness of his Son,* that he might be the firstborn among many brothers and sisters. (Romans 8:29)

The heart of being a disciple boils down to this one thing: God wants us to come to salvation in Jesus and then become more like Jesus to the glory of the Father in the power of the Spirit. For those who want to engage in a deeper dive on the emphasis in these verses and more, we recommend an article by Bobby's colleague Curtis Erskine called "Conversion, Theology, and Discipleship" at Discipleship.org.[14]

Let us explain our core mission from another angle. During our study of the Bible, both of us as authors have sought to understand the underlying teaching of every book in the New Testament on a detailed level. Here is our conclusion: although the circumstances of every book in the New Testament vary for each of the recipients, each book was ultimately written to help people come to faith in Jesus and become more and more like Jesus. If we go back to our definition of a disciple, we can frame it this way: everything was written to help us follow Jesus, be changed by Jesus, and join the mission of Jesus.

Similarly, New Testament scholar Richard Longenecker's book, *Patterns of Discipleship in the New Testament*, shows that the New Testament, in all of its diversity, makes discipleship the major, fundamental, and underlying theme of the entire New Testament.[15] N. T. Wright's *Following Jesus: Biblical Reflections on Discipleship* guides us down a similar path. He puts it this way: "Each writer talks about the life, death, and resurrection of Jesus in order to encourage his readers to follow this Jesus wherever he leads."[16]

Once people orient their hearts to Jesus' way of discipleship, all the weighty questions of life are reframed to include "imitating Jesus" as the core focus. Notice a few examples of the ways in which New Testament writers teach people to follow the ways of Jesus as disciples.

- How do we love people, in the way of Jesus? (John 13:34)
- How do we worship God, in the way of Jesus? (John 4:24)
- How do husbands treat their wives and wives treat their husbands, in the way of Jesus? (Ephesians 5:22–33)
- How do children treat their parents, in the way of Jesus? (Ephesians 6:1–3)

These examples show the numerous challenging situations and difficult circumstances that confront a disciple. But the answer to every situation comes from asking ourselves the same question: How can we follow Jesus and do what Jesus would do in our situation?

The mindset of being a disciple helps us with secondary but vital aspects of the mission of the church community.

Here are four church examples:

- Why does the local church care about the poor? Because we follow Jesus and he cared about the poor.
- Why do we help with our local community? Because Jesus teaches us to love and do good to our neighbors.
- Why do we care about the environment? Because Jesus created the world and put humans over it as stewards.
- Why do we care about racial justice? Because Jesus gives us a new identity and we see everyone through his eyes.

Why were Jesus and the apostles activists for disciple making? If we follow Jesus above all, then we will live like he lived and do what he did in his life, both individually and corporately. But if we overemphasize important causes and neglect our fundamental call to follow Jesus, we will make those secondary things primary. We will not end up with a Jesus-centered life.

Everything written in the New Testament guides us, ultimately, to put on the mind of Christ (1 Corinthians 2:16). In fact, the apostle Paul explained that our formation and obedience to Christ should extend to *each and every thought.*

> We demolish arguments and every pretension that sets itself up against the knowledge of God, *and we take captive every thought to make it obedient to Christ.* (2 Corinthians 10:5)

DeYoung and Gilbert's comprehensive study *What Is the Mission of the Church?* deals with many of the complicated questions about the mission or purpose of the church that thoughtful people ask. These authors thoroughly discuss the role of the kingdom of God, service to the poor, and the place for peace in the church. This is an important book for church leaders to read, especially for young leaders. The two authors sum up their findings in a simple statement: "The mission of the church—your church, my church, the church in Appalachia, the church in Azerbaijan, the church anywhere—is to make disciples of Jesus Christ in the power of the Spirit to the glory of God the Father."[17]

Please take a moment to note an important and practical implication from this chapter. Because disciple making is the core mission of the church, it should invoke a key question for every activity in the church: How does this activity help us to be disciples and make disciples? In this way, church leaders make sure that everything in the church has a clear focus related to the church's core mission.

A disciple making focus keeps the church from less crucial ministries and activities that detract from its mission. It also stops the church from trying to be "everything to everybody." Devoting herself to too many unnecessary activities can distract the local church from her core mission. We must keep coming back to Jesus and disciple making.

Let's make it practical: we must work hard to make disciple making our true core mission. We have both worked extensively with churches and church leaders, and as we've worked with these leaders, we've landed on definitions that many leaders have found helpful. A team of national disciple making leaders developed them to help the local church find greater effectiveness as disciple makers. As you read these definitions, ask yourself, *What would it take for my home church to understand these definitions and fully function according to them?*

WE MUST WORK HARD TO MAKE DISCIPLE MAKING OUR TRUE CORE MISSION.

a. Disciple: someone who is following Jesus, being changed by Jesus, and is committed to the mission of Jesus (Matthew 4:19).

b. Disciple making: entering into relationships to intentionally help people follow Jesus, be changed by Jesus, and join the mission of Jesus (Matthew 28:18–20).

c. Disciple maker: a disciple of Jesus who enters into relationships with people to intentionally help them follow Jesus, be changed by Jesus, and join the mission of Jesus.

d. Disciple making church: a church whose beliefs, habits, and narrative focus on disciple making to such an in-depth level that it quickly becomes clear to everyone, including newcomers, that disciple making is the mission of this church.

We invite you to join us by using these definitions (see Appendix A for additional help). A disciple making focus will energize and give life to every group and church which adopts it. This invitation leads us to our next question: With a church *committed* to this kind of disciple making, what kind of results are possible?

REFLECTION & DISCUSSION QUESTIONS

1. Why is it important to define the core mission of the church? If someone asked you what the core mission of the church is, how would you respond?

2. Prior to this teaching, what did you think was the core mission of the church?

3. If you lived out Colossians 1:28–29 (cited in this chapter), what would God ask you to change?

_____

_____

_____

_____

_____

_____

_____

4. What areas of your life have you totally turned over to the ways of Jesus? What areas still need to be examined?

_____

_____

_____

_____

_____

_____

5. The goal of the church is to make disciples of
   Jesus. How is your church doing with this goal?

_____

_____

_____

_____

_____

_____

6. What is your role in the local church with regard
   to helping it become a disciple making church?
   What's God asking you to do as a next step?

_____

_____

_____

_____

_____

_____

_____

4

WHAT IS THE RESULT OF DISCIPLE MAKING?

Answer: Disciple making results in a church that grows fruitfully and loves generously.

After this I looked, and there before me was
a great multitude that no one could count,
from every nation, tribe, people and language,
standing before the throne and before the
Lamb. They were wearing white robes and
were holding palm branches in their hands.
— Revelation 7:9

Jesus told a parable in Matthew 25:14–30 about a master who went on a trip. Before going away, the master entrusted three of his servants with money to invest and grow while he was in a far country (interestingly, the specific currency was called a "talent"). Upon his return, the master asked each of his servants to give an account of what they had produced by using what he had entrusted to them. Two of the servants approached the master with great joy and showed him how they had doubled their money by investing, but the third hid his entrusted money by burying it in the ground. When this third servant showed the master his unearthed and uninvested "talent," the master went berserk, saying, "You wicked, lazy servant!" (Matthew 25:26). He cast that servant out of his house and distributed his talents to the servants who had produced results.

This story reveals a simple truth: God cares about results.

Yet when it comes to disciple making, defining results can be a mixed bag. Jesus warned disciple makers of this challenge when he told the first of a string of parables in Matthew 13 often called the "kingdom parables." This string of parables could just as well be called the "Parables of Disciple Making," for they string together the major issues and questions

GOD CARES ABOUT RESULTS.

facing serious disciple makers of any age. Take, for example, the first parable, which involves a farmer scattering seed.

> A farmer went out to sow his seed. As he was scattering the seed, some fell along the path, and the birds came and ate it up. Some fell on rocky places, where it did not have much soil. It sprang up quickly, because the soil was shallow. But when the sun came up, the plants were scorched, and they withered because they had no root. Other seed fell among thorns, which grew up and choked the plants. Still other seed fell on good soil, where it produced a crop—a hundred, sixty or thirty times what was sown. Whoever has ears, let them hear. (Matthew 13:3–9)

Jesus' parable reveals how our disciple making efforts will always lead to mixed results. As we see in this parable, disciple makers sometimes scatter seed in places not ready to receive it, not ready to embrace it fully, and not ready to make room for it to thrive. Many will choose to enjoy the seed as a snack a few Sundays a month when they happen to be staying in town on the weekends, but they never embrace the message of discipleship. Others we invite into a discipling relationship might start off with great fanfare and amazing spiritual growth, but for them, their journey ends up being a short-lived fad with no roots. Still others make a serious and heartfelt commitment to following Jesus—but their decision is just one among *many* priorities in their busy and overscheduled lives. Over time, the thorns and thistles of material endeavors in life begin to choke out the nutrients and block out the sunlight needed for fully devoted followers of Jesus to thrive. With all these scenarios, Jesus reminds disciple makers they will always encounter apparent setbacks: people merely wanting a snack on a drive-thru Sunday visit, people who start strong but treat discipleship like a fad, and people too busy chasing anything and everything other than the disciple's life.

Yet disciple makers need not get too discouraged! Jesus closes with a description that makes our disciple making efforts worth it: "Still other seed fell on good soil, where it produced a crop—a hundred, sixty or thirty times what was sown" (Matthew 13:8). Disciples fully trained become "like their teacher" (Luke 6:40). And "like their teacher," they also make disciples, who, when fully trained, then make disciples. Paul explained it to Timothy this way: "And the things you have heard me say in the presence of many witnesses entrust to reliable people who will also be qualified to teach others" (2 Timothy 2:2). A single life fully devoted to Jesus as a disciple maker wins, by the Spirit's power, thirty, sixty, maybe even a hundred more disciple makers. The method of the Master multiplies and multiplies—and the results are staggering.

This parable is important for leaders in the church. As Jesus focused his time and energy raising up "fourth-soil" people—those who produce great fruit—wise leaders similarly seek to raise up "fourth-soil" disciple makers.[18] Leaders in healthy disciple making churches learn to follow Jesus and focus their efforts on raising up these type of disciple makers.

GROWING FRUITFULLY

IN ANOTHER FARMING PARABLE found in Mark's Gospel, Jesus describes the multiplication process in a way that credits the unseen power of God.

> This is what the kingdom of God is like. A man scatters seed on the ground. Night and day, whether he sleeps or gets up, the seed sprouts and grows, though he does not know how. All by itself the soil produces grain—first the stalk, then the head, then the full kernel in the head. As soon as the grain is ripe, he puts the sickle to it, because the harvest has come. (Mark 4:26–29)

By the unseen, miraculous working of God, the seed planted by disciple makers sprouts, grows, multiplies, and produces a harvest. A bumper crop of disciples in one location produces a harvest of disciple makers larger than any storehouse or church can hold. So instead of building a bigger barn, those disciple makers venture out to cast the seeds of discipleship on fresh soil in both local church plants and internationally through missions.[19]

This multiplication is not merely theoretical; multiplying disciples produces a multiplication of disciple making and church planting. It is exciting to hear about these movements springing up around the globe.[20] The results are amazing. Imagine the results of one disciple maker.

- One disciple maker wins 30 disciple makers to the Lord Jesus in a lifetime . . .
- And those 30 disciple makers each win 30 to the Lord Jesus in a lifetime . . .
- And those 900 disciple makers each win 30 to the Lord Jesus in a lifetime . . .
- And those 27,000 disciple makers each win 30 to the Lord Jesus in a lifetime . . .
- And those 810,000 disciple makers each win 30 to the Lord Jesus in a lifetime . . .
- And those 24.3 million disciple makers each win 30 to the Lord Jesus in a lifetime . . .

- And those 729 million disciple makers each win 30 to the Lord Jesus in a lifetime . . .
- And those 2.187 billion disciple makers each win 30 to the Lord Jesus in a lifetime . . .

If this happened, the entire planet would have the opportunity to become fully devoted followers of Jesus in about eighty years. While the parable of the sower teaches us that the math will break down because not everyone will positively respond, there is great encouragement to be found in the reality of what happens when disciples make disciples. This kind of multiplication, in the power of the Holy Spirit, gives us a vision of how to win many in the world for Christ in our lifetime. But exponential growth is just a small portion of the actual results that would follow.

LOVING GENEROUSLY

Jesus taught us another clear result of being a disciple: "By this everyone will know that you are my disciples, if you love one another" (John 13:35). What kind of love sets Jesus' disciples apart? Jesus described it as loving one another "as I have loved you" (John 13:34). This went beyond politeness and niceness to being the kind of profuse, generous love Jesus

GENEROUS LOVE IS THE SIGNATURE CARD OF A TRUE DISCIPLE.

kept showing until it culminated in his sacrificial death on the cross. Generous love is the signature card of a true disciple. Kelvin Teamer provides a good definition of Christlike love: "Love is a cross-shaped action that glorifies God and benefits someone else."[21]

The New Testament repeatedly emphasizes the centrality of love for how we treat people (e.g., Mark 12:31; Colossians 3:14; 1 John 3:23). The apostle Paul explained that the three greatest attributes of a disciple are faith, hope, and love—yet the greatest is love (1 Corinthians 13:13). In everything a disciple does, love should be the driving force. And put in the context of a local body of believers, a disciple making church loves like Jesus.

Jesus spoke another parable in Matthew 25 about sheep and goats. The sheep represent the fully devoted followers (the same idea as those who come from the "good soil"). The life of each sheep has a multiplying impact for good in the world. Disciples that are trained as "kingdom-first" people actually do more good for state and nation than anyone else. Jesus implied that the results of disciple making would be seen in changed lives, reshaped communities, compassionate ministries for those at the margins, and a heightened awareness of the value of every person as the image of God or even as the hidden image of Jesus himself.

Look at Jesus' words:

> Then the King will say to those on his right,
> "Come, you who are blessed by my Father; take
> your inheritance, the kingdom prepared for you
> since the creation of the world. For I was hungry
> and you gave me something to eat, I was thirsty
> and you gave me something to drink, I was a
> stranger and you invited me in, I needed clothes
> and you clothed me, I was sick and you looked
> after me, I was in prison and you came to visit me."
>
> Then the righteous will answer him, "Lord, when
> did we see you hungry and feed you, or thirsty and
> give you something to drink? When did we see you
> a stranger and invite you in, or needing clothes and
> clothe you? When did we see you sick or in prison
> and go to visit you?"
>
> The King will reply, "Truly I tell you, whatever you
> did for one of the least of these brothers and sisters
> of mine, you did for me." (Matthew 25:34–40)

Disciple making produces nothing less than world change. This result is the ultimate answer to praying the Lord's Prayer, "Your kingdom come, your will be done, on earth as it is in heaven" (Matthew 6:10). As C. S. Lewis explained, "If you read history you will find that the Christians who did most for the present world were just those who thought most of the next."[22]

But even that is still not the end of the story for disciple makers who make other disciple makers. Imagine if the prayers of the saints on earth were multiplied thirty, sixty, or a hundred-fold. What would that do to the unfolding will of our Almighty God? Prayer is far more powerful than we typically assume from our earthly vantage point. We read in Revelation 8 that in response to the prayers of God's people came "peals of thunder, rumblings, flashes of lightning and an earthquake" (v. 5).

The church on earth is made up of disciple makers who pray and change the world. In cooperation with their efforts, God holds back evil, lifts oppression, thwarts violence, and eliminates famines and plagues. Angels gather up the prayers of the saints with the incense of God's holiness and take them up to heaven where they are heard—and then hurl them back to earth as "reversed thunder." These prayers "reenter history with incalculable effects. Our earth is shaken daily by it."[23]

Do you long to see generous love and fruitful growth inside the church which changes the world outside the church? Are you willing to spend time on your knees asking God to make it so? Are you willing to arrange your schedule to become a disciple maker whom God uses to answer your prayer?

God uses serious disciple makers to alter history and shape eternities, all by his grace and power. Disciple making churches love generously and experience fruitful growth. Now, practically speaking, what does this look like in a fallen world?

REFLECTION & DISCUSSION QUESTIONS

1. Why do you think God cares about the results of our disciple making efforts?

2. Read Matthew 13:3–9 and notice how the various types of soils are described. How might you describe your spiritual journey to someone in the terms of these types of soils?

3. Churches which raise up disciple makers see fruitful growth. How could this practically be accomplished in the local church?

4. Kelvin Teamer's definition of Christlike love is "a cross-shaped action that glorifies God and benefits someone else." What's an example of this kind of love you've seen in action?

5. Give some examples of love shown through disciple makers in your own local church.

_____

_____

_____

_____

_____

_____

6. When churches grow fruitfully and love generously, the world changes. This week, what's the next step you can take on your disciple making journey?

_____

_____

_____

_____

_____

_____

5

HOW DO DISCIPLES LIVE IN THIS WORLD?

Answer: Disciples of Jesus live in the world but are not of it. They are distinctive even as they permeate a dark world with light.

The kingdom of heaven is like treasure hidden in a field. When a man found it, he hid it again, and then in his joy went and sold all he had and bought that field.
— Matthew 13:44

The poster child for counter-cultural living in almost every way was John the Baptist. He dressed strangely, wearing camel skins and a broad belt, ate an odd diet—devouring locusts and wild honey—and lived without concern for political correctness—denouncing the religious leaders of his time and confronting the immoral marriage arrangement of the king. John also called his disciples to live countercultural lives as well—not calling them to adopt his style of clothing or diet, but to live counterculturally.[24] John explained to the crowds that their heritage as Jews could not save them. Instead, each person must produce the fruit of a repentant life committed to being a fully devoted God-follower. When asked what this type of repentance looked like, he got specific. He said, "Anyone who has two shirts should share with the one who has none, and anyone who has food should do the same." To tax collectors he said, "Don't collect any more than you are required to." Then, to soldiers he said, "Don't extort money and don't accuse people falsely—be content with your pay" (Luke 3:11–14).

John's model of discipleship instructs disciples to give sacrificially as needs arise and be willing to share half of their wardrobe to help another find dignity. He directed those with food to share their table, their pantry, and their smokehouse in order to provide for those going without. Behind these actions, his disciples were to maintain an attitude of contentment, being satisfied with enough and not harboring an insatiable desire to acquire more. Fairness in the treatment of others was to mark those who held power, and honesty and integrity were to be displayed in every human interaction. John the Baptist called his followers into a countercultural life of service to others as they strove to be fully devoted God-followers. When John the Baptist transferred some of his followers over to Jesus (John 1:29–31), they found in their new disciple making leader one who not only lived counterculturally but also one who stood against the culture to transform it.[25]

DON'T BE AFRAID OF DIFFERENT

In Jesus' greatest message, the Sermon on the Mount, the tone remains countercultural from the beginning and throughout. He opens his message describing what it means to live the "blessed life," with language that opposed the values their culture would suggest—spiritual poverty, mourning, meekness, purity, peacemaking, mercy-giving, and joy in accepting persecution. Upon completion of these countercultural "Beatitudes" (Matthew 5:3–12), Jesus then laid out his vision for how a disciple should live in the world.

> You are the salt of the earth. But if the salt loses its saltiness, how can it be made salty again? It is no

longer good for anything, except to be thrown out and trampled underfoot. You are the light of the world. A town built on a hill cannot be hidden. Neither do people light a lamp and put it under a bowl. Instead, they put it on its stand, and it gives light to everyone in the house. In the same way, let your light shine before others, that they may see your good deeds and glorify your Father in heaven. (Matthew 5:13–16)

Simply put, Jesus' disciples should live so dynamically, so boldly, and so brightly that their lives elevate and illuminate everything in the world around them.

Salt does that. Just as salt adds flavor to a bland meal, disciples add the spice of life to real living—showing a confused world where to turn for the meaning of life. As salt preserves food from decay and putrefaction, disciples keep the world from falling further into chaos and destruction. By living counterculturally to everyone around them, disciples renew the world by renewing the teachings of Jesus.

DISCIPLES RENEW THE WORLD BY RENEWING THE TEACHINGS OF JESUS.

We live in a time where it can be easy to lose our saltiness. In fact, the Laodicean church in Revelation showed what happens when "salt" loses its saltiness. The Lord described the church this way:

> I know your deeds, that you are neither cold nor hot. I wish you were either one or the other! So, because you are lukewarm—neither hot nor cold—I am about to spit you out of my mouth. You say, "I am rich; I have acquired wealth and do not need a thing." But you do not realize that you are wretched, pitiful, poor, blind and naked. (Revelation 3:15–17)

There was nothing countercultural, nothing salty, about them. They were rich, proud, self-assured, and confident, but Jesus saw them only as completely pitiable. There were no distinguishing markers of kingdom life. The salt had lost its saltiness. The church had become indistinguishable from her surroundings. Using disciple making language, it appears that the church was filled with converts but not disciples. The Laodicean Christians were followers lacking in the substance of authentic discipleship.

If a Christian is being discipled into a lifestyle that looks indistinguishable from the world, something is fundamentally wrong. "Different" is to be expected. In fact, the meaning of the word "holy"—which describes God *and* his people—means "set apart." True disciples live as salt and light. We keep our distinctive differences (our "saltiness") even as we permeate darkness with

TRUE DISCIPLES LIVE AS SALT AND LIGHT.

light. When we lose our distinctive "saltiness," we lose our effectiveness as "light." Both are necessary for disciples of Jesus. We cannot reach people of the world by living lives indistinguishable from them. Therefore, Jesus tells us that true disciples arrange their lives around countercultural priorities.

- True disciples abide in the Word of God (John 8:31).
- True disciples love one another sacrificially (John 13:34–35).
- True disciples bear fruit—such as love, joy, and peace—which the world craves but cannot produce (John 15:7–8).

Wholehearted followers of Jesus live differently from the world but are respected by many in the world simply because followers of Jesus know what they believe, they know how to love, and the character of their lives is compelling enough to win the respect of outsiders.

START WITH PRAYER

THERE IS SOMETHING ELSE important to note about Jesus' disciple making. He uniquely relied on the power of God through prayer and fasting. Jesus started his ministry by first spending forty days fasting and praying (Matthew 4:1–11). Then during his ministry, he regularly withdrew to pray privately (Mark 1:35). And when he had a monumental decision to make that would determine the success of his entire ministry, it was so critical he spent the entire night in fervent prayer discussing the matter repeatedly with his Father (Luke 6:12).

The life of prayer that marked Jesus' life and preceded his invitation to disciple making became the foundation stone of the earliest disciple making practices as well. As early as the first chapter of Acts, the church "joined constantly in prayer" (Acts 1:14), and prayer both preceded and empowered important decisions. In Jesus' own ministry, notice that it was after a night of prayer that he selected the Twelve.

> When morning came, he called his disciples to him and chose twelve of them, whom he also designated apostles: Simon (whom he named Peter), his brother Andrew, James, John, Philip, Bartholomew, Matthew, Thomas, James son of Alphaeus, Simon who was called the Zealot, Judas

son of James, and Judas Iscariot, who became a traitor. (Luke 6:13–16)

From this motley crew of twelve—less a traitor—Jesus would influence the entire world. His vision was to reconcile fallen humanity to God through himself and restore them to their original image and glory.

FOCUS ON A FEW

How would Jesus fulfill this magnificent vision to redeem the world? Surprisingly, his process entailed raising up a handful of followers and molding them into disciples who make disciples, who then make disciples. His values centered around relationship, imitation, practical experience, service, and multiplication. He gave three years of his life to invest in relationships with the Twelve; he gave special attention to the Three (Peter, James, and John); and he found in the young apostle John a confidant and close friend for his own journey. Look at the math; it's all small numbers: three years and twelve disciples. Yet it worked.

Jesus focused his time and energy upon a few concentric circles, which allowed him to invest himself fully into the lives of a few, allowing them to become imitators of himself. John's Gospel tells us, "God so loved the world that he gave his one and only Son" (John 3:16). But each Gospel also shows that Jesus so loved the world that he invested his greatest energy and largest amount of time impressing his life upon a few close followers whom he believed could then disciple others. Notice this is exactly the opposite of the focus of most contemporary churches. Let us explain what we mean.

Imagine a bullseye target. Then, think of each concentric circle working out from the bullseye as a level of relationship Jesus had with people. One could say Jesus had great relationships at every level of the target.

- Level One: one-to-one with John (John 19:26).
- Level Two: one-to-three with Peter, James, and John (Matthew 17:1).
- Level Three: one-to-twelve with the apostles (Matthew 10:2–4).
- Level Four: one-to-seventy-two with the disciples on the "Limited Commission" (Luke 10:1).
- Level Five: one-to-five hundred to whom Jesus appeared after the resurrection (1 Corinthians 15:6).
- Level Six: one-to-thousands (or multitudes) in settings such as the Sermon on the Mount (Matthew 5:1).[26]

Jesus focused *most* of his attention upon Levels One to Three, while most modern churches focus their primary focus upon Levels Four to Six. The problem with this overemphasis on Levels Four to Six is that converts are typically made at Levels Four to Six but disciples are typically formed at Levels One to Three.

The following diagram contrasts the two models.

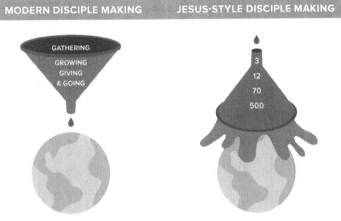

Source: Emotionally Healthy Discipleship

Jesus so loved the whole world that he wanted to save it—which required him to focus on just a few.

In my book *Discipleship that Fits*, I (Bobby) and my co-author, Alex Absalom, note a slightly different model based on social spaces in which Jesus formed his disciples.[27] There is the public context (e.g., Jesus and the crowds); social context (e.g., Jesus and the Seventy-Two); personal context (e.g., Jesus and the Twelve); transparent context (e.g., Jesus and the Three); and the divine context (e.g., Jesus and the Father). Each context is important, and none should be neglected. Yet it is important to remember that Jesus spent most of his focused attention on the smaller contexts. In other words, he focused on just a few, and it paid off.

In Jesus' disciple making parables of Matthew 13, two of them explain his strategy of focusing on smaller things in order to produce maximum results.[28] It is counterintuitive to think small, but there is a hidden truth in small things Jesus probably learned from helping around the house or in the yard. Jesus revealed the truth this way:

> The kingdom of heaven is like a mustard seed, which a man took and planted in his field. Though it is the smallest of all seeds, yet when it grows, it is the largest of garden plants and becomes a tree, so that the birds come and perch in its branches." He told them still another parable: "The kingdom of heaven is like yeast that a woman took and mixed into about sixty pounds of flour until it worked all through the dough. (Matthew 13:31–33)

Jesus knew that the secret to "impressive" results was multiplication. Multiplication required Jesus to focus on a different formula for lasting results rather than his "massive gatherings" that often stemmed from one of his miracles that gathered a crowd. Make no mistake, Jesus could and would draw, entertain, and engage a crowd—and leave everyone spellbound. Jesus sometimes did massive feats. But to change the world, he regularly and intentionally kept his focus on the small size of gatherings—the best for disciple making. We recommend church leaders follow Jesus' lead here by implementing the same focus for their ministry. In Appendix A, we provide some key resources that will help you focus on a few.

WHY SMALLER THINGS?

THE MIDDLE EASTERN MUSTARD seeds of Jesus' day, which still exist today, were about the size of a poppy seed—almost impossible to hold between two fingers because they were so small. But when planted in the ground, the smallest of all garden seeds produced a bush large enough—some thirty feet high with a twenty-foot spread—that it is more often called a tree. The North American bush with similar results is the crepe myrtle that grows so large that at some point, once again, a bush must then be called a tree.

Jesus' parable of the mustard seed is incredibly encouraging. This small seed is potent and powerful enough to make a huge impact. After all, the potency of a small seed does not lie in the gardener's skill but in the Creator's genius. In the same way, the potency of disciple making is unlocked by God's Spirit. The gardener plants the potent seed into the ground, yielding massive results that would be unimaginable from such a tiny beginning. The power of this small seed is that it grows to such heights and stability—then becomes the gathering place for others.

When churches are intentional about making disciples who make disciples, the increase can create a hundred-fold movement of the Spirit, bringing a fresh harvest that can sweep through a nation. Jesus believed that investing in a few was the secret to exponential growth, but will churches follow his lead? Will church leaders want the results badly enough to think and strategize differently? Return once again to the disciple making parables of Matthew 13 and notice the courageous acts of bold people who carry this kind of entrepreneurial spirit in their approach to the kingdom.

> The kingdom of heaven is like treasure hidden in a field. When a man found it, he hid it again, and then in his joy went and sold all he had and bought that field. Again, the kingdom of heaven is like a merchant looking for fine pearls. When he found one of great value, he went away and sold everything he had and bought it. (Matthew 13:44–46)

Churches that make disciples who make disciples value the disciple making mission of Jesus above all other practices. When the leadership of a church returns to disciple making as its core mission, it values making disciples who make disciples over every program that might exist in their church. The disciple making, exponentially multiplying kingdom is the treasure hidden in a field that must be purchased and the pearl of greatest price that must be obtained.

Disciple making church leaders shepherd with the goal in mind, knowing that one day, they will give an answer for their congregation as to why it was filled with converts but so few disciples making disciples. Jesus closes the disciple making parables with a reminder of how each life, each kingdom believer, will be judged.

> Once again, the kingdom of heaven is like a net that was let down into the lake and caught all kinds of fish. When it was full, the fishermen pulled it up on the shore. Then they sat down and collected the good fish in baskets, but threw the bad away. This is how it will be at the end of the age. The angels will come and separate the wicked from the righteous and throw them into the blazing furnace, where there will be weeping and gnashing of teeth. (Matthew 13:47–50)

One day Jesus will likely ask churches why they gathered so many crowds, yet produced so few disciples. Jesus concluded his parables with a reminder that the stakes are high, and that the one casting the net is looking for good fish to gather and keep.

WHAT PRICE ARE WE WILLING TO PAY?

WE WANT TO END this chapter by describing the legacy left by the apostle John.[29] It comes to us from the writings of church father Clement of Alexandria, who lived AD 150–215. This ancient tradition tells us that John left his exile on the Island of Patmos after the death of a tyrant emperor named Domitian and returned to Ephesus to serve the churches of Asia. John, now an old man, lived in the surrounding cities, where he helped appoint elders and set churches in order. In one city not too far away, John saw a young man, "powerful in body, handsome in appearance and ardent in faith." John entrusted the young man to the leaders of the church and said, "This youth I commit to you in all earnestness, in the presence of the Church and with Christ as a witness." One of the church leaders in particular accepted the charge from John to disciple this young man and took personal responsibility for his growth. Taking the young man into his home, this elder reared, kept, and finally baptized him. The young man grew as a disciple under the guiding influence of the elder, but after some time the elder relaxed his disciple making posture, assuming the seal of the Lord would keep the boy in secure protection.

Eventually, he began hanging around youths who led him into moral laziness, wild parties, and even crime. Before long, he was joining these friends at night in highway robberies. The young man soon gave up on his walk with God. He seemed to be once again lost, and he lived as a rebel. Forming a band of robbers, the talented young man became the captain of the bandits—even becoming the fiercest, bloodiest, and cruelest of them all.

Time passed, and the apostle John returned to the province to check up on the churches. While there, he inquired of the elder entrusted with the responsibility to disciple the young man: "Restore to us the deposit which Jesus and I committed to you in the presence of the Church."

The church leader was at first confused, thinking that it was a false charge about stolen money. But when John explained that he was referring to the young man, the church leader, groaning deeply and bursting into tears, said, "He is dead."

"How and what kind of death?" John replied.

"He is dead," he said, "to God. For he turned wicked and abandoned the faith, and is now a robber. He and his band of robbers have taken possession of the mountain in front of the church."

John tore his clothes in lament and then called for a horse. John rode away, just as he was, straight from the church. When John arrived at the foot of the mountain, the robbers' outpost, they arrested him. The apostle neither fled nor complained, but cried out, "It was for this I came. Take me to your captain."

When the young bandit leader recognized John, he turned, ashamed, and tried to run. The old man followed with all his might, forgetting his age, and cried out:

> Why, my son, do you flee from me, your spiritual father? Fear not; there is still hope for you. I will give account to Christ for you. If need be, I will willingly endure death, as the Lord did die for us. For your sake, I will surrender my life. Stand and believe, for Christ has sent me.

The young man threw down his arms, trembled, and began to weep bitterly. The old man approached, embraced him, and baptized him again. The man then reengaged in the life of a disciple with the apostle John as his teacher. Through a life of copious prayers, continual fasting, and the renewal of his mind with the Word of God, the young man was restored to the church. His life became a model of true repentance, a token of regeneration, and a trophy of the hope all have in the resurrection of Jesus.

Even in his old age, John was a disciple maker to the very end. His core mission was the mission of Jesus: making disciples. This hard and costly work combined the Great Commandment *and* the Great Commission. The Apostle of Love knew that a life that loves both God and people will make disciples. Then, that disciple likewise disciples yet others, who in turn disciple others. Each disciple maker stands in a holy line of world-changers. Looking toward the front of that long line, we see such heroes as Moses, Elijah, and Hannah, not to mention Peter, Paul, Priscilla—and many others. And at the very front of the line is the Lamb whom they are all following.

> They follow the Lamb wherever he goes. They were purchased from among mankind and offered as firstfruits to God and the Lamb. (Revelation 14:4)

May God grant you a legacy of joining the long line of disciple makers. The line of disciples-who-make-disciples curves its way through every culture and every age, connecting us to the great reformers, church fathers, apostles, and even to Jesus himself. Our desire for you—when you close your eyes at the end of your life and reflect upon what your life has been all about—is that you will think of the people you have discipled to become Jesus-followers. You will feel the same way Paul felt about those he discipled.

> For what is our hope, our joy, or the crown in which we will glory in the presence of our Lord Jesus when he comes? Is it not you? Indeed, you are our glory and joy. (1 Thessalonians 2:19–20)

Are you convinced that disciple making is the core mission of the church? Are you ready to make it *your* core mission? We urge you to make a specific and concrete decision right now, by taking these four actions steps:

1. Determine if making disciples will be a core personal mission for your life.
2. Make a commitment to God about this new priority in your life through prayer, as you ask for his help in order to make the commitment a reality.
3. Review the recommended resources in Appendix A.
4. Meet with a leader(s) from your church to enlist their help explicitly so that, with their support, you make your commitment a reality. If the leaders from your church cannot help you, find someone outside your church who will help you.

1. How would you describe to a new believer what it means to live counterculturally?

_____

_____

_____

_____

_____

_____

2. In what area of your life are you most concerned about living counterculturally (work, marriage, raising kids, church life, etc.)?

_____

_____

_____

_____

_____

_____

3. What would it mean for you to be "salt" (as described in Matthew 5:13) in your everyday life (work, home, play)?

_____

_____

_____

_____

_____

_____

4. Describe some of the sacrifices that people have made to be disciples and make disciples. You can draw these from the Bible or early church tradition, as described above.

_____

_____

_____

_____

_____

_____

_____

5. What risks or sacrifices do you need to make in order to become a disciple who makes disciples?

_____

_____

_____

_____

_____

_____

6. Are you ready to make the commitment to disciple making as described at the end of the chapter? If not, consider fasting and prayer for: 1) the Holy Spirit to show you what it would take to become a disciple maker and 2) the Holy Spirit to show you who should disciple you or whom you should disciple. Write out your commitment or prayer here.

_____

_____

_____

_____

_____

POSTSCRIPT

A PARABLE OF URGENCY

King Hezekiah, king of the Jews in the seventh century BC, feared the Assyrians would lay siege to the royal city of Jerusalem over which he ruled. He also feared a season of starvation and slow death would be brought upon Jerusalem's inhabitants. Hezekiah knew the primary water source for the city, the Gihon Spring, was located outside the city walls and was protected only by a guard tower. The spring lay vulnerable to attack by Sennacherib, the cruel dictator of Assyria, and its water could be easily diverted by Sennacherib's soldiers to supply the enemy. Hezekiah acted quickly.

> It was Hezekiah who blocked the upper outlet of the Gihon Spring and channeled the water down to the west side of the City of David. He succeeded in everything he undertook. (2 Chronicles 32:30;

see also 2 Kings 20:20; 2 Chronicles 32:2–4; Isaiah 22:11)

Hezekiah accomplished his mission by designing an aqueduct that would channel all the water of the Gihon into a tunnel, known today as "Hezekiah's Tunnel," and from there into the Pool of Siloam.[30] His mission-critical decision brought life-giving sustenance to the people of God.

But how did he accomplish this great feat? According to the Siloam Inscription,[31] found at the halfway mark inside the 583-yards-long ancient tunnel, we learn about the method he employed (for reference, a cubit is approximately 20 inches):

> And this is the story of the tunnel while . . . the axes were against each other and while 3 cubits were left to cut . . . and on the day of the tunnel being finished the stonecutters struck each man towards his counterpart, axe against axe and flowed water from the source to the pool for 1,200 cubits. And 100 cubits was the height over the head of the stonecutters.[32]

The mission was vital to the life of the community, and the people gave it the highest priority. The project was carried out in teams working from different directions toward the same goal. Each team involved skilled stonecutters, trained by earlier generations in the use of an axe and chisel. And each stonecutter had others working alongside him, assisting and also carrying out the rock and debris. The teams used the best math and technology of their day, but also trusted in their own wisdom and intuition. At the most critical point of the venture, they had to listen to one another, come together, and work toward a common cause that would save them all. When the last strike of the axe landed its blow, water came rushing forth. The tunnel has been a steady supply of water for the city now for more than 2,800 years.

Many people were saved by Hezekiah's focus on the mission. He did not give in to fate, nor did he shirk back from a big challenge. He led and his people followed. They overcame the enemy's siege.

Satan has laid siege to our civilization. To survive and thrive, we must act quickly; for us in the West, this is a mission-critical moment as the culture continues its slide into post-Christian secularism. Jesus, as our king, has given us the mission of bringing living water to our culture, our communities, and our congregations. To do so, we must employ Jesus' strategy for Jesus' mission. This moment in Western history will call us to work in teams, learn from our craftsman, use the latest research, engage the latest technology, employ age-old wisdom, and listen to the voice of him calling us to come together.

King Jesus is calling us to make disciples—his core mission for the church—and join him in this exciting journey. Unless Jesus' core mission becomes again our core mission, the siege-works of the enemy will overwhelm the faithful and the civilization will be led off into spiritual captivity. The King is calling his disciple-makers to pick up their axes, rally their followers, and usher in a season when living water flows upon the land.

APPENDIX A

KEY DISCIPLE MAKING RESOURCES

Ten Key Books on Disciple Making for Church Leaders

1. David Young, *King Jesus and the Beauty of Obedience-Based Discipleship* (Grand Rapids: Zondervan, 2020).
2. Jim Putman, Bobby Harrington, and Robert Coleman, *DiscipleShift: Five Shifts That Help Your Church to Make Disciples Who Make Disciples* (Grand Rapids: Zondervan, 2013).
3. Robert Coleman, *The Master Plan of Evangelism*, 2nd ed. (Grand Rapids: Revell, 2006).

4. Bobby Harrington and Alex Absalom, *Discipleship that Fits: The Five Kinds of Relationships God Uses to Help Us Grow* (Grand Rapids: Zondervan, 2016).

5. Brandon Guindon, *Disciple Making Culture: Cultivate Thriving Disciple-Makers Throughout Your Church* (Nashville: HIM Publications, 2020).

6. Will Mancini and Cory Hartman, *Future Church: Seven Laws of Real Church Growth* (Grand Rapids: Baker Books, 2020).

7. Bill Hull, *The Disciple-Making Pastor: Leading Others on the Journey of Faith*, rev. ed. (Grand Rapids: Baker Books, 2007).

8. Bobby Harrington and Josh Patrick, *The Disciple Maker's Handbook: Seven Elements of a Discipleship Lifestyle* (Grand Rapids: Zondervan, 2017).

9. Peter Scazzero, *Emotionally Healthy Discipleship: Moving from Shallow Christianity to Deep Transformation* (Grand Rapids: Zondervan, 2021).

10. Jim Putman and Chad Harrington, *The Revolutionary Disciple: Walking Humbly with Jesus in Every Area of Life* (Nashville: HIM Publications, 2021).

Six Content Resources to Use in Disciple Making

1. Bobby Harrington, *Trust and Follow Jesus: Discipleship Conversations* (Renew.org, 2019).

2. Bobby Harrington, *Trust and Follow Jesus: Discipleship Conversations: The Leader's Guide* (Renew.org, 2020).

3. Bobby Harrington, *Starting a Transparency Group Using the Teachings of Jesus*, renew.org/ebook/starting-a-discipleship-group.

4. Discovery Bible Study: dbsguide.org.

5. Jim Putman, Bill Kraus, Avery Willis, Brandon Guindon, *Real-Life Discipleship Training Manual*, Teacher's Guide ed. (Colorado Springs: NavPress, 2010).

6. James Bryan Smith and Richard Foster, *A Spiritual Formation Workbook: Small Group Resources for Nurturing Christian Growth*, rev. ed. (San Francisco: HarperOne, 2010).

Church Coaching

The Relational Discipleship Network specializes in helping churches make the shift toward a disciple making focus. See rdn1.com for more information.

APPENDIX B

RENEW.ORG NETWORK LEADERS' VALUES AND FAITH STATEMENTS

Mission: We Renew the Teachings of
Jesus to Fuel Disciple Making

Vision: A collaborative network equipping
millions of disciples, disciple makers, and
church planters among all ethnicities.

SEVEN VALUES

RENEWAL IN THE BIBLE and in history follows a discernible outline that can be summarized by seven key elements. We champion these elements as our core values. They are listed in a sequential pattern that is typical of renewal, and it all starts with God.

1. *Renewing by God's Spirit.* We believe that God is the author of renewal and that he invites us to access and join him through prayer and fasting for the Holy Spirit's work of renewal.

2. *Following God's Word.* We learn the ways of God with lasting clarity and conviction by trusting God's Word and what it teaches as the objective foundation for renewal and life.

3. *Surrendering to Jesus' Lordship.* The gospel teaches us that Jesus is Messiah (King) and Lord. He calls everyone to salvation (in eternity) and discipleship (in this life) through a faith commitment that is expressed in repentance, confession, and baptism. Repentance and surrender to Jesus as Lord is the never-ending cycle for life in Jesus' kingdom, and it is empowered by the Spirit.

4. *Championing disciple making.* Jesus personally gave us his model of disciple making, which he demonstrated with his disciples. Those same principles from the life of Jesus should be utilized as we make disciples today and champion discipleship as the core mission of the local church.

5. *Loving like Jesus.* Jesus showed us the true meaning of love and taught us that sacrificial love is the

distinguishing character trait of true disciples (and true renewal). Sacrificial love is the foundation for our relationships both in the church and in the world.

6. *Living in holiness.* Just as Jesus lived differently from the world, the people in his church will learn to live differently than the world. Even when it is difficult, we show that God's kingdom is an alternative kingdom to the world.

7. *Leading courageously.* God always uses leaders in renewal who live by a prayerful, risk-taking faith. Renewal will be led by bold and courageous leaders—who make disciples, plant churches, and create disciple making movements.

TEN FAITH STATEMENTS

WE BELIEVE THAT JESUS Christ is Lord. We are a group of church leaders inviting others to join the theological and disciple making journey described below. We want to trust and follow Jesus Christ to the glory of God the Father in the power of the Holy Spirit. We are committed to *restoring* the kingdom vision of Jesus and the apostles, especially the *message* of Jesus' gospel, the *method* of disciple making he showed us, and the *model* of what a community of his disciples, at their best, can become.

We live in a time when cultural pressures are forcing us to face numerous difficulties and complexities in following God. Many are losing their resolve. We trust that God is gracious and forgives the errors of those with genuine faith in his Son, but our desire is to be faithful in all things.

Our focus is disciple making, which is both reaching lost people (evangelism) and bringing people to maturity (sanctification). We seek to be a movement of disciple making leaders who make disciples and other disciple makers. We want to renew existing churches and help plant multiplying churches.

1. *God's Word.* We believe God gave us the sixty-six books of the Bible to be received as the inspired, authoritative, and infallible Word of God for salvation and life. The documents of Scripture come to us as diverse literary and historical writings. Despite their complexities, they can be understood, trusted, and followed. We want to do the hard work of wrestling to understand Scripture in order to obey God. We want to avoid the errors of interpreting Scripture through the sentimental lens of our feelings and opinions or through a complex re-interpretation of plain meanings so that the Bible says what our culture says. Ours is a time for both clear thinking and courage. Because the Holy Spirit inspired all sixty-six books, we honor Jesus' Lordship by submitting our lives to all that God has for us in them.

> *Psalm 1; 119; Deuteronomy 4:1–6; 6:1–9;*
> *2 Chronicles 34; Nehemiah 8; Matthew 5:1–7:28;*
> *15:6–9; John 12:44–50; Matthew 28:19; Acts 2:42;*
> *17:10–11; 2 Timothy 3:16–4:4; 1 Peter 1:20–21.*

2. *Christian convictions.* We believe the Scriptures reveal three distinct elements of the faith: *essential* elements which are necessary for salvation; *important* elements which are to be pursued so that we faithfully follow Christ; and *personal* elements or opinion. The gospel is *essential.* Every person who is indwelt and sealed by God's Holy Spirit because of their faith in the gospel is a brother or a sister in Christ. *Important* but secondary elements of the faith are vital. Our faithfulness to God requires us to seek and pursue them, even as we acknowledge that our salvation may not be dependent on getting them right. And thirdly, there are personal matters of opinion, disputable areas where God gives us personal freedom. But we are never at liberty to express our freedom in a way that causes others to stumble in sin. In all things, we want to show understanding, kindness, and love.

> *1 Corinthians 15:1–8; Romans 1:15–17;*
> *Galatians 1:6–9; 2 Timothy 2:8; Ephesians 1:13–14;*
> *4:4–6; Romans 8:9; 1 Corinthians 12:13;*
> *1 Timothy 4:16; 2 Timothy 3:16–4:4;*

Matthew 15:6–9; Acts 20:32; 1 Corinthians 11:1–2; 1 John 2:3–4; 2 Peter 3:14–16; Romans 14:1–23.

3. *The gospel.* We believe God created all things and made human beings in his image, so that we could enjoy a relationship with him and each other. But we lost our way, through Satan's influence. We are now spiritually dead, separated from God. Without his help, we gravitate toward sin and self-rule. The gospel is God's good news of reconciliation. It was promised to Abraham and David and revealed in Jesus' life, ministry, teaching, and sacrificial death on the cross. The gospel is the saving action of the triune God. The Father sent the Son into the world to take on human flesh and redeem us. Jesus came as the promised Messiah of the Old Testament. He ushered in the kingdom of God, died for our sins according to Scripture, was buried, and was raised on the third day. He defeated sin and death and ascended to heaven. He is seated at the right hand of God as Lord and he is coming back for his disciples. Through the Spirit, we are transformed and sanctified. God will raise everyone for the final judgment. Those who trusted and followed Jesus by faith will not experience punishment for their sins and separation from God in hell. Instead, we will join together with God in the renewal of all things in the consummated kingdom. We will live

together in the new heaven and new earth where we will glorify God and enjoy him forever.

> *Genesis 1–3; Romans 3:10–12; 7:8–25;*
> *Genesis 12:1–3; Galatians 3:6–9; Isaiah 11:1–4;*
> *2 Samuel 7:1–16; Micah 5:2–4; Daniel 2:44–45;*
> *Luke 1:33; John 1:1–3; Matthew 4:17;*
> *1 Corinthians 15:1–8; Acts 1:11; 2:36; 3:19–21;*
> *Colossians 3:1; Matthew 25:31–32; Revelation 21:1ff;*
> *Romans 3:21–26.*

4. *Faithful faith.* We believe that people are saved by grace through faith. The gospel of Jesus' kingdom calls people to both salvation and discipleship—no exceptions, no excuses. Faith is more than mere intellectual agreement or emotional warmth toward God. It is living and active; faith is surrendering our self-rule to the rule of God through Jesus in the power of the Spirit. We surrender by trusting and following Jesus as both Savior and Lord in all things. Faith includes allegiance, loyalty, and faithfulness to him.

> *Ephesians 2:8–9; Mark 8:34–38; Luke 14:25–35;*
> *Romans 1:3, 5; 16:25–26; Galatians 2:20;*
> *James 2:14–26; Matthew 7:21–23; Galatians 4:19;*
> *Matthew 28:19–20; 2 Corinthians 3:3, 17–18;*
> *Colossians 1:28.*

5. *New birth.* God so loved the world that he gave his one and only Son, that whoever believes in him shall not perish but have eternal life. To believe in Jesus means we trust and follow him as both Savior and Lord. When we commit to trust and follow Jesus, we express this faith by repenting from sin, confessing his name, and receiving baptism by immersion in water. Baptism, as an expression of faith, is for the remission of sins. We uphold baptism as the normative means of entry into the life of discipleship. It marks our commitment to regularly die to ourselves and rise to live for Christ in the power of the Holy Spirit. We believe God sovereignly saves as he sees fit, but we are bound by Scripture to uphold this teaching about surrendering to Jesus in faith through repentance, confession, and baptism.

> *1 Corinthians 8:6; John 3:1–9; 3:16–18; 3:19–21; Luke 13:3–5; 24:46–47; Acts 2:38; 3:19; 8:36–38; 16:31–33; 17:30; 20:21; 22:16; 26:20; Galatians 3:26–27; Romans 6:1–4; 10:9–10; 1 Peter 3:21; Romans 2:25–29; 2 Chronicles 30:17–19; Matthew 28:19–20; Galatians 2:20; Acts 18:24–26.*

6. *Holy Spirit.* We believe God's desire is for everyone to be saved and come to the knowledge of the truth. Many hear the gospel but do not believe it because they

are blinded by Satan and resist the pull of the Holy Spirit. We encourage everyone to listen to the Word and let the Holy Spirit convict them of their sin and draw them into a relationship with God through Jesus. We believe that when we are born again and indwelt by the Holy Spirit, we are to live as people who are filled, empowered, and led by the Holy Spirit. This is how we walk with God and discern his voice. A prayerful life, rich in the Holy Spirit, is fundamental to true discipleship and living in step with the kingdom reign of Jesus. We seek to be a prayerful, Spirit-led fellowship.

> *1 Timothy 2:4; John 16:7–11; Acts 7:51;*
> *1 John 2:20, 27; John 3:5; Ephesians 1:13–14;*
> *5:18; Galatians 5:16–25; Romans 8:5–11;*
> *Acts 1:14; 2:42; 6:6; 9:40; 12:5; 13:3; 14:23; 20:36;*
> *2 Corinthians 3:3.*

7. *Disciple making.* We believe the core mission of the local church is making disciples of Jesus Christ—it is God's plan "A" to redeem the world and manifest the reign of his kingdom. We want to be disciples who make disciples because of our love for God and others. We personally seek to become more and more like Jesus through his Spirit so that Jesus would live through us. To help us focus on Jesus, his sacrifice on the cross, our unity in him, and his coming return, we typically share

communion in our weekly gatherings. We desire the fruits of biblical disciple making which are disciples who live and love like Jesus and "go" into every corner of society and to the ends of the earth. Disciple making is the engine that drives our missional service to those outside the church. We seek to be known where we live for the good that we do in our communities. We love and serve all people, as Jesus did, no strings attached. At the same time, as we do good for others, we also seek to form relational bridges that we prayerfully hope will open doors for teaching people the gospel of the kingdom and the way of salvation.

> *Matthew 28:19–20; Galatians 4:19;*
> *Acts 2:41; Philippians 1:20–21; Colossians 1:27–29;*
> *2 Corinthians 3:3; 1 Thessalonians 2:19–20;*
> *John 13:34–35; 1 John 3:16; 1 Corinthians 13:1–13;*
> *Luke 22:14–23; 1 Corinthians 11:17–24; Acts 20:7.*

8. *Kingdom life.* We believe in the present kingdom reign of God, the power of the Holy Spirit to transform people, and the priority of the local church. God's holiness should lead our churches to reject lifestyles characterized by pride, sexual immorality, homosexuality, easy divorce, idolatry, greed, materialism, gossip, slander, racism, violence, and the like. God's love should lead our churches to emphasize love as the distinguishing sign of

a true disciple. Love for one another should make the church like an extended family—a fellowship of married people, singles, elderly, and children who are all brothers and sisters to one another. The love of the extended church family to one another is vitally important. Love should be expressed in both service to the church and to the surrounding community. It leads to the breaking down of walls (racial, social, political), evangelism, acts of mercy, compassion, forgiveness, and the like. By demonstrating the ways of Jesus, the church reveals God's kingdom reign to the watching world.

> *1 Corinthians 1:2; Galatians 5:19–21;*
> *Ephesians 5:3–7; Colossians 3:5–9;*
> *Matthew 19:3–12; Romans 1:26–32; 14:17–18;*
> *1 Peter 1:15–16; Matthew 25:31–46;*
> *John 13:34–35; Colossians 3:12–13; 1 John 3:16;*
> *1 Corinthians 13:1–13; 2 Corinthians 5:16–21.*

9. *Counter-cultural living.* We believe Jesus' Lordship through Scripture will lead us to be a distinct light in the world. We follow the first and second Great Commandments where love and loyalty to God come first and love for others comes second. So we prioritize the gospel and one's relationship with God, with a strong commitment to love people in their secondary points of need too. The gospel is God's light for us. It teaches us

grace, mercy, and love. It also teaches us God's holiness, justice, and the reality of hell which led to Jesus' sacrifice of atonement for us. God's light is grace and truth, mercy and righteousness, love and holiness. God's light among us should be reflected in distinctive ways like the following:

A. We believe that human life begins at conception and ends upon natural death, and that all human life is priceless in the eyes of God. All humans should be treated as image-bearers of God. For this reason, we stand for the sanctity of life both at its beginning and its end. We oppose elective abortions and euthanasia as immoral and sinful. We understand that there are very rare circumstances that may lead to difficult choices when a mother or child's life is at stake, and we prayerfully surrender and defer to God's wisdom, grace, and mercy in those circumstances.

B. We believe God created marriage as the context for the expression and enjoyment of sexual relations. Jesus defines marriage as a covenant between one man and one woman. We believe that all sexual activity outside the bounds of marriage, including same-sex unions and same-sex marriage, are immoral and must not be condoned by disciples of Jesus.

C. We believe that Jesus invites all races and ethnicities into the kingdom of God. Because humanity has exhibited grave racial injustices throughout history, we believe that everyone, especially disciples, must be proactive in securing justice for people of all races and that racial reconciliation must be a priority for the church.

D. We believe that both men and women were created by God to equally reflect, in gendered ways, the nature and character of God in the world. In marriage, husbands and wives are to submit to one another, yet there are gender specific expressions: husbands model themselves in relationship with their wives after Jesus' sacrificial love for the church, and wives model themselves in relationship with their husbands after the church's willingness to follow Jesus. In the church, men and women serve as partners in the use of their gifts in ministry, while seeking to uphold New Testament norms which teach that the lead teacher/preacher role in the gathered church and the elder/overseer role are for qualified men. The vision of the Bible is an equal partnership of men and women in creation, in marriage, in salvation, in the gifts of the Spirit, and in the ministries of the church but exercised in ways that honor gender as described in the Bible.

E. We believe that we must resist the forces of culture that focus on materialism and greed. The Bible teaches that the love of money is the root of all sorts of evil and that greed is idolatry. Disciples of Jesus should joyfully give liberally and work sacrificially for the poor, the marginalized, and the oppressed.

> *Romans 12:3–8; Matthew 22:36–40;*
> *1 Corinthians 12:4–7; Ephesians 2:10;*
> *4:11–13; 1 Peter 4:10–11; Matthew 20:24–27;*
> *Philippians 1:1; Acts 20:28; 1 Timothy 2:11–15;*
> *3:1–7; Titus 1:5–9; 1 Corinthians 11:2–9;*
> *14:33–36; Ephesians 5:21–33; Colossians 3:18–19;*
> *1 Corinthians 7:32–35.*

10. *The end.* We believe that Jesus is coming back to earth in order to bring this age to an end. Jesus will reward the saved and punish the wicked, and finally destroy God's last enemy, death. He will put all things under the Father, so that God may be all in all forever. That is why we have urgency for the Great Commission—to make disciples of all nations. We like to look at the Great Commission as an inherent part of God's original command to "be fruitful and multiply."

We want to be disciples of Jesus who love people and help them to be disciples of Jesus. We are a movement of disciples who make disciples who help renew existing churches and who start new churches that make more disciples. We want to reach as many as possible—until Jesus returns and God restores all creation to himself in the new heaven and new earth.

Matthew 25:31–32; Acts 17:31; Revelation 20:11–15; 2 Thessalonians 1:6–10; Mark 9:43–49; Luke 12:4–7; Acts 4:12; John 14:6; Luke 24:46–48; Matthew 28:19–20; Genesis 12:1–3; Galatians 2:20; 4:19; Luke 6:40; Luke 19:10; Revelation 21:1ff.

NOTES

1. C. S. Lewis, *Mere Christianity* (San Francisco: Harper Collins, 2001), 199.

2. Renew.org Network and Discipleship.org are both national and international disciple making ministries. Bobby serves as the co-founder and point leader of both ministries. Renew.org's mission is to "renew the teachings of Jesus to fuel disciple making" and discipleship.org's mission is to "champion Jesus-style disciple making." Renew.org upholds specific teachings whereas discipleship.org is a broader evangelical network. Both organizations feature some of the same leaders. Both share the same conviction that disciple making is the core mission of the church. Where possible, like this instance, we will use definitions that all the many ministry leaders, scholars, and practitioners involved with Discipleship.org vetted out. See https://discipleship.org/about-discipleship-org/.

3. The word *Shema* is the Hebrew word for "hear," which is also the first word of Deuteronomy 6:4. Hearing

and passing along these truths were crucial to the future faithfulness of succeeding generations in Israel. These verses from Deuteronomy are the most recited and formative verses in Judaism even to this day.

4. For more on the Deuteronomy 6 model of disciple making, see Jason Houser, Bobby Harrington, and Chad Harrington, *Dedicated: Training Your Children to Trust and Follow Jesus* (Grand Rapids: Zondervan, 2015).

5. David Young, *King Jesus and the Beauty of Obedience-Based Discipleship* (Grand Rapids: Zondervan, 2020).

6. The commands of Jesus are the commands of the whole Bible. *Real Life Theology: Fuel for Faithful and Effective Disciple Making* (Renew.org, 2021) emphasizes this concept.

7. For more on this idea, see Matthew Bates, *The Gospel Precisely* (Renew.org, 2021) and Matthew Bates, *Gospel Allegiance* (Grand Rapids: Brazos, 2019).

8. For the gold-standard description of Jesus' disciple making model, see Robert Coleman, *The Master Plan of Evangelism*, 2nd ed. (Grand Rapids: Revell, 2006).

9. For more information on this definition and how to use it, see Jim Putman, Bobby Harrington, and Robert Coleman's book, *DiscipleShift: Five Steps That Help Your Church to Make Disciples Who Make Disciples* (Grand Rapids: Zondervan, 2013).

10. For more information, see Bobby Harrington and Josh Patrick, *The Disciple Maker's Handbook: Seven Elements of a Discipleship Lifestyle* (Grand Rapids: Zondervan, 2017).

11. The exact percentage of time that Jesus spent focused on discipling the Twelve is hard to peg, but this is commonly quoted. Dave Ferguson quotes 73 percent as a good number, see https://churchleaders.com/pastors/pastor-articles/320680-essential-practices-leaders-multiply-leaders-carey-nieuwhof-dave-ferguson.html, accessed March 3, 2021.

12. Rick Warren, *The Purpose Driven Church: Growth Without Compromising Your Message and Mission*, rev. ed. (Grand Rapids: Zondervan, 2010).

13. For further development on how disciple making encompasses all the major functions of church, see Jim Putman, Bobby Harrington, and Robert Coleman, *DiscipleShift: Five Steps That Help Your Church to Make Disciples Who Make Disciples* (Grand Rapids: Zondervan, 2013).

14. Curtis Erskine, "Conversion, Theology, and Discipleship," Discipleship.org, accessed March 18, 2021, https://discipleship.org/bobbys-blog/conversion-theology-discipleship/.

15. See Richard Longenecker, *Patterns of Discipleship in the New Testament* (Grand Rapids: Wm. B. Eerdmans, 1996).

16. N. T. Wright, *Following Jesus: Biblical Reflections on Discipleship*, rev. ed. (Grand Rapids: Wm. B. Eerdmans, 2014).

17. Kevin DeYoung and Greg Gilbert, *What Is the Mission of the Church? Making Sense of Social Justice, Shalom, and the Great Commission* (Wheaton: Crossway, 2011), 265.

18. For more information on Jesus' method, see Robert Coleman, *The Master Plan of Evangelism*, 2nd ed. (Grand Rapids: Revell, 2006).

19. On the topic of building "bigger barns," see Jesus' parable about the rich fool who kept building more and more properties but gave no thought to eternity (Luke 12:16–21).

20. For a summary description of disciple making in the USA and disciple making movements, see "National Study on Disciple Making in USA Churches: High Aspirations Amidst Disappointing Results, 2020" by Discipleship.org and Exponential.org, prepared by Grey Matter Research & Consulting: https://discipleship.org/national-study-on-disciple-making-in-usa-churches/.

21. See the volume in this series called *Kingdom Life: Experiencing God's Reign Through Love and Holiness* by Kelvin Teamer (Renew.org, 2021).

22. C. S. Lewis, *Mere Christianity* (San Francisco: Harper San Francisco, 2001), 134–135.

23. Eugene Peterson, *Reversed Thunder: The Revelation of John and the Praying Imagination* (San Francisco: Harper San Francisco, 1988), 88. The phrase "reversed thunder" is a phrase that originates with the poet George Herbert.

24. See Carol Swain, *Counter-Cultural Living: What Jesus Has to Say About Life, Marriage, Race, Gender Identity, and Materialism* (Renew.org, 2021).

25. For a classic understanding of this issue, see H. Richard Niebuhr, *Christ & Culture* (New York: Harper & Row, 1951). The author has a helpful discussion of Jesus' five responses to the challenges of culture by the church.

26. See Milton Jones, *Discipling: The Multiplying Ministry* (Ft. Worth: Star Bible, 1982), 80–84, for the best treatment of this concept. Jones credits Gary Collins, *How To Be a People Helper* (Santa Ana: Vision House, 1976) for these categories.

27. Bobby Harrington and Alex Absalom, *Discipleship that Fits: The Five Kinds of Relationships God Uses to Help Us Grow* (Grand Rapids: Zondervan, 2016).

28. Churches that have added a small group strategy to their church have experienced a growth built around community, relationship, and full-member participation. However, the next step for a church that wishes to multiply is to think smaller by investing in a few. Often, this means that the idea is to focus on discipleship groups of

three or four where everyone fits around a table at a local restaurant or park.

29. Clement of Alexandria, "Who Is the Rich Man Who Can Be Saved?" (Section *XLII*, trans. William Wilson) in Vol. 2 of *Ante-Nicene Fathers,* eds. Alexander Roberts, James Donaldson, and A. Cleveland Coxe (Buffalo: Christian Literature Publishing Co., 1885). Some of the quotes have been modernized in language.

30. Jesus would later send the blind man of John 9 to this pool to wash and be healed.

31. Interestingly, it was while snorkeling in the tunnel that a young boy named Jacob Eliahu Spafford found the inscription. He was the adopted son of Horatio Spafford who wrote, "It Is Well With My Soul."

32. Gary Rendsburg and William Schniedewind, "The Siloam Tunnel Inscription: Historical and Linguistic Perspectives," *Israel Exploration Journal*, 60, no. 2 (2010): 188–203. *Research with Rutgers.*